M000104997

# SISTERS BY HEART
# PARTNERS IN AGING

*Best wishes!*
*Maryhen Fuller*

# SISTERS BY HEART
# PARTNERS IN AGING
## A MEMOIR OF TWO WOMEN

BY

## MARY LOU FULLER

§

LINE DRAWINGS BY JIM DUGAN

EDITED BY KAY AMSDEN

§ *Kay Amsden*

KALM PUBLISHING COMPANY
DURHAM, NEW HAMPSHIRE

ALSO BY MARY LOU FULLER

*A HORSE IN THE LADIES' ROOM*
*WHERE LAME DONKEYS LIE*
*ON THE WINGS OF A UNICORN*

DEDICATED TO THE EXCEPTIONAL QUALITIES
OF STRENGTH, LOVE AND SPIRITUALITY SHARED BY WOMEN
OF ALL AGES

COPYRIGHT © 2001

BY

MARY LOU FULLER


REQ  KALM Publishing                                    :
149 East Side Drive
Concord, NH 03301
uniqueyankee@comcast.net

ISBN: 0-9657894-3-8


§

ALL RIGHTS RESERVED. NO PART OF THIS PUBLICATION MAY BE REPRODUCED
STORED IN A RETRIEVAL SYSTEM OR TRANSMITTED IN ANY FORM OR BY ANY
MEANS - ELECTRONIC, MECHANICAL, PHOTOCOPY, RECORDING OR ANY OTHER
EXCEPT FOR BRIEF QUOTATIONS IN PRINTED REVIEWS, WITHOUT THE PRIOR
PERMISSION OF THE PUBLISHER

We are two women who value the presence of each other in our
lives

We are two women who feel good about being women; who
honor our experiences and are moved to share them

We are two women unfolding the fabric of our friendship to take
a look at the threads that weave it together

§

The warm pastels of caring
The shadowy darkness of crisis and disagreement
The brilliant gold of shared sunrises
The greens of growth and understanding
The purples of risk-taking
The reds of passion
The blues of serenity found under God's Heaven and beside His
still waters
The earth tones of peace and contentment
The knowledge that rather than wither on the vine in our
seventies, we are ripening into springtimes still to be shared

MLF

# MAKING FRIENDS WITH THE AVON LADY

*"...aging is like driving a car: it seems you're just doing 30, then you're pushing 40 and suddenly before you can hit the brakes, you're at 55..."*
                                                                Anonymous

## A Chance Meeting

As I knelt on the bathroom floor carrying out my weekly devotions to toilet bowl cleaning, I heard the unmistakable sound of tires rolling up the gravel lane to my cabin. The business-like slam of the car door told me instantly it was no one I knew.

I groaned to my feet and peered out the window to see who had happened on my woodland hideaway. There was talk in the village about an Avon Lady cruising around town and I said to myself, "Damn! It's her. Way out here too. What nerve."

The tall, slim, angular figure approached the front steps. I muttered again, "Gawd. She's a piss-poor ad for beauty products." Then seeing her determined expression and the deep furrow between her eyes I made a quick re-assessment: "I was right the first time: piss-poor looks for Avon; probably sells encyclopedias."

When I opened the door, I received no ESP that my life would change forever once this woman crossed my threshold. She was to become the Gibraltar in my life, my partner and cohort in twenty years-worth of challenges that would reverse the sand in the hour glass. Although our chronological ages would stubbornly advance, with each new adventure we shed more of the "fear of trying" until ultimately our minds and bodies fed on - and drew vigor from - our endeavors.

Kay introduced herself; her firm handshake further distanced her from Avon country. "I'm looking for Marion Brackett," she said. "I understand she works for you as an au pair."

When I told her Marion moved back to Massachusetts, Kay appeared extremely disappointed. She continued, "I wanted to tell her in person about the death of a mutual friend who taught with me at

UNH. Their acquaintance went back many years to college days." I thought to myself, this person is an academic, not selling encyclopedias *or* Avon.

When it was my turn, I told Kay my children no longer needed an au pair. Amey was thirteen and away at camp. Josh, sixteen, was at his job across the lake at the hotdog stand. I told her the cabin was my summer getaway from our home in the hot city of Keene where I worked and the kids went to school.

"You drove all the way over from Durham just to find Marion?"

"I tried to reach you by telephone but you're unlisted. Marion didn't even know this individual was ill. I thought it would be kinder to tell her in person. Anyway, it's a beautiful day for a drive."

"Well, at least I can give you lunch. It's just a cold meat loaf sandwich. I live pretty simply: tight budget; not many extras in the fridge."

We ate on the deck overlooking the forest of trees that separated my little house from Laurel Lake. I enjoyed my quiet life as much for the peace as to preserve the magic and tranquility of the woods. The birds, chipmunks and squirrels showed off more than usual as they ran up and down trees or chased one another through the gardens and ferns. Even the hummingbird couple bustled in to visit their red feeder. The sun peeked through the leaves and dappled in splotches on the deck. A sudden breeze carried the leafy pattern across Kay's face and reflected in her eyeglasses.

Totally unaware of elapsing time, I found myself sharing with this woman how I came to be where and what I was. She asked intermittent questions in a comfortable tone that turned on my magpie mode and I rattled on.


After the Fitzwilliam Inn

I was currently working in the personnel department of a Keene insurance company and had done so since Red's death. I loved my job, which involved in-house staff training. Because it had a remote similarity to Kay's classroom work, it brought a common denominator into our conversation.

I spoke of the ten years Red and I owned the Fitzwilliam Inn and told her some of the hilarity and hard work so much a part of that business.

"People staying in old inns have no idea what goes on behind the scenes. It's really unbelievable. My husband was a detail junky and

10

kept diaries of everything we encountered. He would say, 'Someday you'll write a book'."

Kay laughed until tears ran unchecked down her face. It was then I noticed how laughing and smiling changed this serious, unadorned woman. As her eyes wrinkled in laughter, the furrow that lived between them was suddenly less pronouced as her forehead became involved in the facial changes a touch of humor brought about. The softening relaxed her entire demeanor and in turn had the same effect on me.

## Percale Walls

Kay had a two-hour drive back to Durham and asked to use the bathroom before she headed out. She must have read the expression on my face as a preamble to a plumbing problem, or that we only had an outhouse, because she hastily said, "That's O.K. I can stop at McDonalds on the way." I told her things weren't *that* bad, but almost.

Purchasing the land had drained my resources, but I was so anxious to have even primitive housing, I only had the cabin's outer shell constructed along with plumbing and wiring.

Plywood floors and no walls would be the mode of living for a long time. That didn't bother me a bit. The decision to build, sensational in and of itself, was my first step in a show of autonomy. Added to that was the exhilarating sense of freedom I experienced just having myself to answer to; another of those "living on the edge" feelings I got from being a newly independent woman. Neither the fifteen abusive years of my first marriage, nor Red's tragic death, could touch me now. I refused to allow what had gone before to throw back dark shadows on the new world I had created for myself and the children.

Leading the way I took Kay on a short tour. I pointed out my Percale walls, a gentler term for sheets hanging everywhere to afford a semblance of privacy. The kids and I were so used to being surrounded by Percale, it wasn't until someone new came in that I thought about how it must look. Well-worn and tattered, I had culled the sheets from the inn linen inventory years before. Destined for a future as rags, here they gave one last measure of faithful service.

The bathroom was "sheeted" especially well. Even so, if the children were in the right mood they delighted in tweaking the sheets to expose a sister or brother stepping out of the shower.

I showed her the loft with its odd flight of stairs. Canted at a stark twenty-five degrees, with a mere four-inch riser space, the ladder

Percale walls

was a last minute substitute for the wrought iron circular staircase originally planned, but the allotted space had proved too small. Now they
resembled an obstacle course reject and required diagrams for ascent
and descent, with WARNING notices at the top and bottom.

My room was on the back with windows opening on two sides.
I told Kay one of my greatest pleasures was being lulled to sleep by the
swaying of the pines and, in the morning light, looking up at birds'
nests in the oak trees. By contrast if I rolled over, I could see through
the studs into the kitchen where I had an unimpeded view of the sink
drainpipes.

As we moved through the house Kay was fascinated by my
dreams for the place. The great cathedral ceiling in the living room was
ringed on one side by the railing that fronted the loft. The rest of the
room was a vast, airy space. The sliding glass doors leading to the deck
gave me a view of the woods and beyond to the skyline of trees that
marched along on the far side of the lake.

"Someday I plan to borrow on the equity and have the house
properly finished. This could easily be a year-round home, three sea-
sons at least. I want a place to live after I retire. I might even start up
the antique business I had in our barn in the village. The shed out back
here is a miniature version of the house, loft and all. It cries out to be
a shop of some kind."

Kay confessed a love of the woods also and reminisced about
the aroma of pines basking in the sun at her family's camp on the
Blackwater River near Contoocook, New Hampshire. We spoke of the
visual pleasure we each drew from the massive granite boulders scat-
tered around my cabin. I told her about the enormous granite ledge
that slept beneath a large part of Fitzwilliam.

These very boulders had been a cause of concern when my
septic system was designed. I had wanted the house positioned to allow a view from the deck of my small piece of waterfront; sadly the
boulders and ledge were in the way. The house had to be turned south-
east several degrees and my view disappeared. "I pay a huge property
tax here. You'd think I owned the water too at the rate of assessment.
A lot of owners rent their cottages for one of the summer months. I
can't bear the thought of anyone else living here; even if that income
*would* pay the taxes."

Kay laughed as I told her another boulder story. Originally the
gravel lane came just to the house. The woods separating the house
from the lake were so dense I tied clothesline from tree to tree to help

13

us find our way to and from the water. Like Hansel and Gretel we followed the rope up and down the hill.

When I decided to continue the road to the water, the rope route was used by the contractor. Unfortunately, the young man doing the work arrived with a bulldozer too small for the job. All attempts failed to push the monoliths out of the way and the result was proof rolling stones *do* gather; the operator leaped to safety seconds before the bulldozer went over an embankment. Meanwhile the boulder rolled victoriously on to a new resting place where it completely blocked further attempts to build the road according to plan. The circumventing detour cost me extra in bulldozer time and surfacing materials.I was certain the boulder developed a smug attitude as we were forced to walk around it. Over the years the contours of our feet wove a single-file path that attracted summer rain and spring runoffs reduced the detour to a state of enduring mud.

A rolling stone does gather

A Friendship Rises

    Kay's visit to the lake that day was over twenty years ago, but I can still recall feeling a special bond would grow out of that chance meeting. We had begun to weave the fabric of a friendship.

    Regretfully the lake house is no longer part of our lives although it remained the focal point of our relationship for over a decade. Now, on nights when I am unable to sleep, I take myself back to that Eden, re-trace the gravel road up to the house until once more I'm on the deck where I sat that first afternoon and watched the taillights on her car disappear around the bend.

    In retrospect I thought about the eagerness with which I told her my amusing stories while, like Peter Pan, I kept the shadows of my past folded in my pocket. I was over fifty and trying to get a life together that gave no hint of self-pity but was centered on all things positive. There were already many plusses: family, home and career being the top three. Still, I lacked adult companionship but knew a third marriage was not the answer.

    Labor Day brought the dreaded move back to Keene. Although I would continue to make weekend trips to the cabin well into fall, the departure from full-time life in the woods was a sad transition.

    Kay made several return trips to the lake. I would have said I had known her much longer than a few months as we explored the commonalities in our thinking, widely interspersed among the vast differences in our backgrounds. She had already worked her way into my thoughts and I was surprised how readily I sought her advice on household and financial matters. She recognized my need for independence but at the same time gave off the subliminal message of support and genuine caring for me and my family.

    Women had been a lifeline in the past but I was aware Kay possessed a degree of strength I had heretofore not experienced.

Over the years Kay and I have frequently exchanged thoughts about those early days when the greens of growth and understanding began to take root. She had told me about the hurt and mental suffering she'd endured when her longtime partner abandoned the life they'd shared together. "I was so angry with myself for not seeing it coming I punched my fist into the wall," she said. "The greatest difficulty was working with her in the same department."

I, on the other hand, had a background of two marriages spread over twenty-five years. One ending in divorce, the second in widowhood. Kay and I were similarly bruised even though each of us carried a different sort of emotional baggage. As a result, our journey together was one of support and strength for each other. We became sisters by heart.

# THE PSYCHOLOGICAL PITFALLS OF TEENS, PIGEONS AND RATS

*"...to make another happy, is to be happy oneself..."*
Anonymous

## Josh's Story

As a child my son Josh had more than a passing interest in all things feminine. He was eight years old the day he loaded my shopping cart with Barbie Doll clothes. When questioned, he said they were for Amey; ever the big brother confederate, she insisted it was true.

The following Christmas, Amey set her sights on a life-size doll head that came with a set of hairdressing tools - combs, scissors and curlers. Anchored to a two-foot stand, its long hair was full of fat pink rollers. Even though Amey was old enough to play with the toy, I felt the choice was not hers alone. As I suspected, on Christmas morning the "head" was barely out of its wrapping when Josh took charge.

My heart went out to my gentle little boy as he explained, "I just want to show her how to use it."

In the ensuing weeks, he spent hours with the "head" - tirelessly washing, curling, styling and combing. Ultimately he cut the hair so many times it was reduced to inoperable fuzz. The fascination was gone. Amey pronounced it "a dead head", held a mock funeral and upended the hapless creature into her toy box.

Years later, now that Kay was a frequent visitor, she and Josh had developed a good rapport. About to enter his junior year at Keene High School, he confided to Kay the grim details of the name-calling and coarse treatment he received from his peers the previous year at the school. He told of lighted cigarettes held to his face, the bodily roughing up he received from the football team and his entrapment at the local pizza hangout where he was threatened with a beating if he refused to obey the lewd orders issued by his tormentors. When he was safe at home he never uttered a word, and I failed to see the hurts

17

he suffered.

I could feel my heart wilt as Kay told me Josh's story. She finished with, "He really shouldn't be forced to return to that school. If you're willing, let me enroll him as a tuition student at the high school in Durham; because of the university, it's a much more open and accepting community."

Josh and I made a trip to Durham. We visited the school and had a candid talk with the guidance personnel. Josh was excited about the environment and the positive attitude of everyone he met. I, on the other hand, was drowning in guilt over my failure to be in tune with the agonies he'd endured in Keene. As I went through the mournful task of signing the enrollment papers listing Kay as his temporary guardian, I was torn between apprehension for the success of the venture and gratitude for Kay's generosity.

The school year began with Amey and me in Keene, Kay and Josh in Durham. It took just three weeks for Kay to realize her PhD, which entitled her to teach young adults, in no way prepared her to oversee a teenager's conformity to even a modicum of rules.

Josh did well in the new school, but his success in classwork paled in comparison to the number of friends he made. Starved for that commodity so long, he was now close to running wild; this was the basis of Kay's problem. Plus she was trying to cope without the parental authority which only comes when one raises a child from the ground up. Her university responsibilities prevented her from maintaining a solid schedule at home which was all the incentive Josh needed to invent his own behavioral guidelines.

In Kay's first phone call about the escalating trouble, she told me, "I came home at 9 p.m. and Josh had not been here; the supper I left in the refrigerator was untouched. No note. No telephone call."

She had spent the hours from 9 p.m. to 1 a.m. sitting in the den, huddled in a quilt, waiting. When he finally walked in she angrily vented her frustration and disappointment at his conduct. Psychologically she felt betrayed after all she had tried to do. I assured her it was not her fault, rather a rule of nature that teenagers will be incited to mischief the minute there is any lapse of supervision. It was such a serious breach in trust, the living arrangements became impossible.

Once again I faced a dilemma. How could I bring Josh back to the school in Keene where the administration decried any knowledge of his peers' abusive behavior? How could I sacrifice Amey's security in a school where she was thriving? I spent a week arguing with myself

Josh had two years before graduation. I finally rationalized it would be more harmful to take him from the new school where he was doing well and decided Amey and I would move to Durham. When Josh graduated, we would return to Keene where she could enter high school.

Amey, chronologically still a child, was filled with adult awareness and compassion. I could only imagine what it cost her to trade all things familiar with everything strange and new. We were a sad pair as we packed bags and cartons in preparation for our move.

Forced to resign my position at the insurance company, I kept the door open by committing to part-time work there during the summer.

Merging Lives

I rented my house in Keene and relocated to Durham for what we all thought would be two years.

Kay's house was a large four-bedroom contemporary on the edge of the university campus. Settling into her home and routine was not easy. I constantly felt the presence of the woman who had shared the house in the past. The four cats she lived with were another hurdle. I arrived with three more, plus Bridget, a yellow Labrador retriever. All Kay's cats were "indoor"; mine went out. She was afraid her cats would be terrorized by the dog, but from the very first Bridget tiptoed around the felines so as not to tread on anybody.

Amey gradually worked her way into the middle school where the scholastic level was far superior to Keene's and offered greater potential for challenge.

Lost in what I viewed as an alien environment, I was the unhappy one. I felt sorry for myself and kept repeating, "It's only for two years." I had forfeited sovereignty over all facets of my life. I harbored a resentment toward everything, particularly Kay, who behaved like the professor she was while I felt more and more like the student. Plus, due to my lack of employment, I was managing the household on an ever tightening budget.

I refused to see that she divided her energy between the demands of teaching and helping me adjust at home. The warmth of understanding I thought we shared came and went like fog in the wind. We were silent, each mired in the depths of our own thoughts. We circled around like wrestlers daring one another to utter the first critical word.

19

I shuddered each time I went into the kitchen and saw orange shag carpet covering a large portion of the counters. It was there specifically for the cats because Kay said, "They like to be up off the floor on a soft, nonskid surface." When I found an entire cupboard similarly carpeted it launched us into our first major battle. When I cooled off and looked at things more empathetically, I realized the cats had been her family until we all arrived and the carpeting was a natural thing for her to have done. When I pointed out more counter space was needed to cook for a family of four, the shag disappeared.

There were other things I failed to recognize. One was my own psychological need to get out of the house and find a job so I too would realize some rewards and satisfaction. I knew I would feel better and so would everyone around me. I also realized my attitude was taking its toll on Kay as she continued to give more and more of herself to make me happy. One of the most unselfish and concerned women I ever knew, she never considered happiness had to grow by itself within a person's heart and soul.

The mental hurdle of applying for work, interviewing and learning something new at my age wasn't a problem for me. Adventurous by nature, I was secure in the knowledge I had many skills to offer. My typing was excellent; I had used a typewriter for forty years. I was a proven writer, producer and practiced leader of training programs for staff in the private sector. Ten years as an innkeeper provided extensive experience with people. I was totally autonomous, could work without supervision and never shied away from responsibility.

## Where are you, Sigmund Freud?

I applied at the University of New Hampshire. Almost immediately I was called for an interview in the Psychology Department. The job was eighty-percent time: I would work from September through June. Perfect for the summer commitment to my employer back in Keene.

Psychology was located in Conant Hall, one of the oldest buildings on campus. It showed. An aroma not unlike the odor of an outhouse greeted me inside the large front door. Up a wide staircase a maze of hallways worn by the feet of hundreds of students led to a number of closed doors behind which, I assumed, lurked the faculty.

The scent from the first floor accompanied me as I found my way to the business office. I was interviewed by a young woman who

Billy was cleaning his pigeon coops on the roof

was filled with over-confident superiority. I felt terribly old but knew legally she couldn't ask my age. I was relieved and surprised when she offered me the job. The starting rate of pay was less than the federal minimum wage but I would receive a full-benefit package which was a factor in my decision to accept the offer.

I was introduced to my work area where a gentle drifting of white fell around us like snowflakes. My "leader" dismissed the flurry with a flick of her hand saying, "Oh, don't mind these feathers. That's Billy cleaning his pigeon coops on the roof." I looked up at the large trapdoor and retractable ladder in the ceiling.

I was still young enough to let things bother me like the elusive word "image" and the critical question, "what will people think?" Therefore, I looked at the job as an humiliation and allowed the thought of what my professional life had become to reduce me to tears. I returned to the degrading scene everyday and diligently typed multiple-choice exams on Ditto masters. There was no way to correct a typing error on these without covering myself with the juicy purple ink which left spots and streaks on my hands, arms and clothes.

It's amazing what one can get used to. At first the transition from the businesslike hustle-bustle of the private sector overwhelmed me; then I began to enjoy the slower pace of academe. I found I was a pretty flexible "older worker" and could bend with change quite satis-factorily. I worked in Psychology for three years before I accepted a full-time position elsewhere on campus. During that time I adjusted to pigeon feathers drifting down. I learned the strange odor in the build-ing was the rats in the cellar used by graduate students for metabolic testing. This, I was told, involved feeding them and then "swimming" them in barrels of water to measure the fat burned off. Where had I gotten the impression that psychology was all about Sigmund Freud and Carl Jung? I *had* aged.

Inanimate things put in a box and transported one hundred miles away, then taken out and arranged on new shelves and in new drawers, takes nothing away from them. They have no soft centers; they are inanimate.

A person similarly transported has more to cope with. The effect on the human spirit, psyche and sensitivity is profound as one struggles to fit one's square being into the round hole of a new environment.

I said to Kay, "We have no shared memories or bedrock to anchor us during this emotional upheaval we're going through. Help me." I reached out. Her hand was there. It still is.

# WE HAVE MET OUR MOTHERS AND THEY ARE US

*"...there is a fountain of youth in your mind...learn to tap this source...you will truly have defeated age..."*

Sophia Loren

## Old is Just a Word

The first time I caught my mother looking back at me from the mirror, I made an ugly face to destroy the image and quickly offered a prayer to the god of wrinkles and jowls, "Please. I'm not ready to see myself like that." The reply was immediate, "You're old; get used to it." But I continued to see her watching me, hogging my reflection, whenever I passed a mirror.

One day I read my mother the obituary of a friend who died at sixty-five. "Good for her," Mimi said. "She doesn't have to find out what it's like to get old."

Unprepared with a defense I could only blurt out, "But I'm sixty."

"You are? I'd forgotten." Had she forgotten or was it an attempt to keep me young in her mind?

Twenty years earlier the worries of aging would never have passed her lips, but she was in a nursing home now, had lost control of her life and was forced to abide by decisions I made for her. I was increasingly sandwiched between the needs of my children and those of my mother. The stress threatened to envelop my life. I finally concluded I had three children; the oldest happened to be in her nineties.

## Two Mothers

Kay had an elderly mother also. There were vast differences between the two women. Edie, Kay's mom, had cosmopolitan roots and went to college at a time when the cost of educating a young woman beyond secondary school was thought an enormous waste. Edie, as if to prove that thinking, married shortly after graduation and moved from the urbanity of Yonkers, New York, to the rural world of Hanover, New Hampshire, where her husband taught at Dartmouth. Edie made the transition gracefully, assuming the role of country faculty wife. She even took on the stoic qualities of a native New Englander including a poker face, sly humor and ramrod straight stature.

By contrast, Mimi began life on a small Massachusetts farm, the fifth child in a flock of six. Money was so scarce, at Christmas they had to be content with a new pair of mittens and an orange. In summer they were pushed out of the house to pick blueberries which they sold door-to-door. Mimi married above her "station in life" and moved from her country home to suburban Philadelphia where she struggled with the dubious airs of that society. Always afraid of what people were thinking, she constantly looked over her shoulder and wore herself out rearranging closets lest somehow she be judged on the folding of her bath towels.

When I moved to Durham, our mothers were advancing into their eighties. We refused to allow them to grow old any more than we gave much thought to the accumulation of our own years. Energetically we involved them in holiday celebrations and family trips. Fortunately for Kay and me, the common ground of age brought a measure of compatibility to our mothers' relationship and they were frequent visitors to Durham.

The four bedrooms in Kay's house worked out comfortably for us, but when the mothers arrived, we knew sharing a bedroom was not their thing.

Anyone who has ever dealt with the devastation a teenager can create in a bedroom knows it was easier for Kay and me to give up our beds than to reconstruct the children's quarters.

We decided to camp out on the living room floor and purchased a large blow-up mattress. Packed in a small pouch, it appeared tame enough until we introduced the first shot of air from the exhaust end of the vacuum. As a balloon takes on an internal spirit as air escapes, so did our mattress as air went in. Reduced to hoots of laughter, we flopped and crawled on the floor as one of us wrestled the wayward mattress into submission while the other pursued the air intake valve with the vacuum hose. Two sixty-year old hoydens.

Christmas

We always had a fire in the fireplace on Christmas Eve. Sprigs of laurel on the mantle formed the backdrop for red candles in brass

The mattress took on an internal spirit

candlesticks and gold papier-mâché angels. The firelight was reflected in the colorful glass balls that hung from the enormous tree in the corner.

A fondue supper was a favorite of teenagers and octogenarians alike. Those that could sat on cushions on the floor around the coffee table; those that could not sat on the couch within arm's reach of the goodies that came and went. The meal began with wine or cocktails. In a short time the mothers experienced radical personality changes as the alcohol found their carefully cultivated inhibitions. Warmed by the fireplace, their "just one drink" induced a silliness in the mothers that must have been good for their souls. It was only when the fondue pot appeared with shrimp, chunks of chicken and beef that their imbibing became apparent.

The mothers' attempts to "bait" their fondue forks was all it took to elicit smothered guffaws from the teenagers. When food dropped off their forks and into the sizzling oil, we were all consumed with laughter, including the mothers. One of us would jump up to rescue the wayward morsel amid shouts of "kiss everyone; you have to kiss everyone." We followed the original rules of fondue which dictated if food drops into the oil the owner must circle the table and kiss "every member assembled".

Josh's senior year was the last holiday we were all together in Durham. It was also the year he discovered the treasures waiting in the local thrift shop. A serious trend-setter in clothing fads, he raided the racks driven by the need to make a new fashion statement, but lacked the funds to purchase first-run items. The result was a conglomeration in which he clothed himself from the skin out; shoes and hats from the 1940's now joined the more established preppy clothes already in his closet.

That Christmas he put on a fashion show for the mothers. Slinking down the stairs, he made a giant leap into the living room. With outstretched arms he shouted, "Ta-Da", then turned and strutted through the room modeling one outrageous combination of cast-offs after another. The mothers shut their eyes in mock agony. The show-stopper was long johns, flowered boxer shorts, boots, sweater two sizes too large, black scarf and beret. Edie's conservative nature was overcome.

She showed her disgust with a loud sniff and said, "I for one would never wear used clothes. What about germs?"

Josh, endowed with a glib tongue which regularly talked him in

28

"Ta-Da"

and out of trouble, turned to Edie with a clever sales pitch about the value and style of his thrift clothes. Had he been an ice cube salesman in the Yukon, and she an Eskimo housewife, his entire stock would have disappeared into her igloo.

There are some moments that live forever in one's mind and this was one. Wearing the old black beret on her soft white curls, a used and tired scarf draped around her diminutive figure, Edie took Josh's arm and proudly showed off her "new" clothes with the same pride as the fabled Emperor.

Motivation

During my fifties it became extremely important for me to keep my mother active and functioning. She had helped us at the inn for ten years; it became her life and her world. When that era ended, she was as lost as I was. Perhaps the motivation ran deeper, and my desire to stay young was reflected in my need to keep Mimi that way also.

Osteoarthritis was the villain in her life. At first she maneuvered with the help of a cane and my arm. I took her on occasional weekend jaunts to places on Cape Cod. She had always enjoyed one of the large hotels at Silver Beach in Falmouth. But the distances across large lobbies and long hallways were too taxing. I rented a cottage in Dennisport which was more satisfactory. With the children's help, she succeeded in getting to the beach and managed to stand in the shallow water where it splashed on her aching knees. As the gentle waves drifted in and out around her ankles, the shifting sand mired her feet deeper and deeper. The children's cries for help brought me dashing across the beach. Mimi was unable to move her legs at all. On my command of "lift", three pairs of arms responded and we hauled my mother back from the clutches of quicksand. She summarized the event with the comment, "Sand didn't move like that in my day."

I drove her down to Herring Cove beach in Provincetown, a spectacular spot on the Cape, with a parking lot right at surfside. I thought it would be perfect for her: just a few feet to the beach and the chair I provided.

"I'm not sitting out there with all those 'homo' people," she declared. Finally, hidden behind dark glasses and a scarf that swathed her head and most of her face, she agreed to sit in the chair. It was clear she felt protected by her disguise. In actuality she stood out even more. I could only wonder what she would do if she knew how close

30

to home the "homo" people were.

When we made a trip to the Ocean House in Watch Hill, Rhode Island, I rented a wheelchair which eased the crossing of expansive public areas and corridors. Our room, which had a marvelous view of sea and sand, was half a flight up from the last stop on the elevator. Not fazed in the least, Mimi sat down and bumped up on her bottom.

Edie, on the other hand, still drove her own car, one of the last in her circle of friends to do so. She was in her fortieth year as a volunteer at Mary Hitchcock Memorial Hospital in Hanover. A fifteen-year breast cancer survivor, she was a tiny powerhouse, possessed of a secret strength evidenced by her stoic independence.She never telephoned for help, even waited until a pre-arranged fall visit to bring the lining of her all-weather coat for Kay to zip in. I chuckled about it and told Kay, "She only does it to make you feel important."

"No," was the emphatic reply, "she just isn't mechanically minded. My father always did that for her. Now that he's gone, I'm the zipper substitute." Although she was beginning to take on some of her mother's aging patterns, Kay refused to admit it, saying, "I'm my father's daughter." She had followed him into teaching and it was from him she had inherited her logical mind and great common sense.

## Onward, Good Daughters

Our last hurrah was a late September excursion to Ledgeland in Sugar Hill, New Hampshire. Both in our sixties, we were born to older mothers who were now approaching ninety. Neither of them had ever experienced the need to keep *their* mothers young and moving. What was it with us? The "handwriting on our wall" told us, "You have been weighed in the balance and found capable; onward, good daughters. Onward." So here we went again jollying our mothers into more adventure than they probably ever wanted.

The drive up to the White Mountains any time is sensational. This time was no exception as we experienced the sun lighting the treetops, the shadows of clouds sliding across the mountains, ski runs carved in their faces. Everywhere we looked there was an animation of color only a New England fall can display. The panorama of red, orange and yellow maples, set against the dark green of the pines, spread further across the landscape with each bend in the highway.

At Ledgeland, we carefully unloaded the mothers and their valises and then, because we were all looking forward to lunch at Polly's famous Pancake Parlor, Kay and I hurried to empty the rest of the car.

"Where's my hanging bag?" I asked.

"Where's *mine?*" was the reply.

"I didn't bring it in."

"Neither did I."

"Where *are* they then?"

"*Damn!* Back in Durham hanging in the kitchen waiting to be put in the car."

"Right."

We looked down at ourselves to see what we would be wearing for the next forty-eight hours. We had planned two evening meals out at nice restaurants in the area; plus two picnics and rides down Attitash on the Alpine Slide. The clothes hanging back in the kitchen had been carefully selected for these activities.

"You're too old to work without a checklist," I told Kay bitterly as I looked at the old khaki slacks I had worn just to ride in the car. They already bagged at the knees. My bitterness was quickly replaced with hysterical laughter as I saw what she had to live in - a pair of cast-off yellow corduroys from Goodwill that ended inches above the tops of her socks.

As it turned out, our pants did get baggier and dirtier but we weren't turned away at any eating places nor were we asked to eat in the kitchen.

The highlight of the trip was a picnic at the base of Mt. Washington. We had packed our cooler with devilled eggs, crackers and cheese, wine, ham sandwiches and slabs of chocolate cake for dessert. We ate surrounded by the aura of the mountain with the cross-hatching of the Cog Railway tracks snaking up its side. It seemed we were frozen in time as the view continued as far as the eye could see. The air was clean and clear without the insult of pollutants and, although we said not a word, looking back I am sure mothers and daughters felt they were in a special presence.

Age had nothing to do with it: we were together. Four women. Two running on ahead, two trying to hold them back and keep them young as long as they could. And all of it for no other reason than "a daughter's your daughter for the rest of her life."

Early in our sisterhood each of the mothers expressed their pleasure that Kay and I had someone with whom to share the approaching senior years. In Edie's words, "I'm glad my daughter has you for a friend."

When it happened, losing our mothers was devastating. We had them for so long and were so old ourselves, it seemed we all should have gone on forever. Instead, I found myself mourning the loss of the only person who shared my childhood memories. I longed for just one more talk with my mother.

It was then Kay and I discovered a new dimension in the caring we shared for each other. A hitherto unexperienced gentleness - a pastel softness in the glare of all else in our lives. We had become aging orphans as well as sisters by heart.

# HUMILITY FOR HISTORY'S SAKE

*"...I know a woman in her eighties who won't even purchase green bananas: it could be a bad investment..."*

Anonymous

## A Common Soliloquy

The temperature was over ninety degrees; a hot humid day that sucked the breath out of my lungs and made me lightheaded.

As I bent to pick up the cigarette butts off the grassy interior of the Fitzwilliam town common on this oppressive day, I questioned my motives for being where I was. I'd been on duty for almost twelve nonstop hours. Not all spent picking up butts to be sure; no, there had been other equally strategic assignments for which the Antiques Show Committee thought I was qualified.

Was I so loath to admit that I was sixty and ask for an indoor job? "You have your pride to think of, you know," I said, being careful not to move my lips as I talked to myself. "You don't look over fifty so no one knows your age except you and your body." I recalled a friend's reaction when her speeding violation was reported in the local newspaper. She was insulted to have her name and age broadcast. "Fifty-five years old, doing sixty in a fifty mile per hour zone!" she had sputtered, more upset by the airing of her age than her misdemeanor.

I was a young sixty, not afraid of new challenges, coping with my two teenagers and able to keep lots of things going at once without more than three lists. My whispered soliloquy went on as I wandered the grass, looking for butts, a sun hat offering the only shade.

"Keep your thinking young. Be frank with yourself and know your limits. Pushing to do things better left to younger people is not in your best interest. You need to catch your second wind so you can devote more time to becoming the woman you want to be." So saying I collected my final butt, unhooked the trash bag from my belt and sailed it into the refuse barrel. "That's it for me," I called out to my leader and headed home.

The Old House

When I came to Fitzwilliam over three decades earlier, one of my first encounters with the eccentricites of old age took place outside the house across the road from the inn. I watched an unusual scene unfold: there were two characters and at first their actions and dialogue meant nothing. Gradually I caught on and was amazed at the tenacity of the leading players. The play would ultimately have a bittersweet finale which catapulted me into that task on the common.

The old building and the man living in it appeared to be about the same age. In reality the house was built in 1837; the man was born thirty years later. They had grown to look alike in much the same way people and their pets take on similar features. The house was gray, tired and sagging. Its windows stared blindly at the world, clouded by years of an accumulation of dirt and rain. The old man sagged too. His skin was gray from too many days indoors. His eyes, clouded with cataracts, stared blindly at the world.

Presently a woman arrived. She was younger, a relative term when one is ninety and the other eighty. The woman's spinal curvature brought the ends of her shawl dangerously close to the ground. They might have tripped her but she had lived with herself long enough to

36

know better.

She approached the old man where he stood supported by his cane. "Carrie? Time for my cigar," he shouted in a voice harsh from years of complaining.

"O.K., Roy." The woman turned her body in a single precise movement and headed for the village store thirty yards away. Her curvature kept her off-balance. She had tipped onto her face more than once on these trips; it took her almost an hour to make a complete circuit. She sang a little song as she went, "One, Carrie. Not two, Carrie."

Once upon a time she was asked why she made the trip twice a day and only purchased one cigar at a time. "Because Roy's so tight with a dime he's afraid he might not live to smoke the second one. He'd never leave an unsmoked cigar for someone to find."

Roy Blake died two years later. Perhaps part of his legacy *was* a lone cigar, but by far the most important was the old house - given to the local historical society for a museum.

Under new owners, the building began to take on a fresh spirit. It straightened with pride as the warm caring hands of the society members lovingly cleaned and polished every floorboard and window.

The rooms were restored. Walls were stripped down to the bones of old lath and new plaster applied; no drywall here. The dining room and parlor rugs were washed, repaired and relaid. Wallpaper was hung that closely resembled the original design and texture. Stencilling was added to the walls in the master bedroom. Shelves to exhibit toys were put up in the children's room.

The maintenace of the old house became the society's life, one of love and devotion. Over time, memorabilia, archives and artifacts poured in from families with connections to Fitzwilliam, and the place became a sanctuary and repository for the history of a town.

I was privileged to take a turn as president of the society in those formative days. We had no treasury and a museum over one hundred years old to maintain and nurture. We scrambled to come up with fund-raising ideas. A Strawberry Festival was introduced the same year as the Antiques Show; both provided such an enormous boost to our finances they became annual events. The number of volunteers required for these lucrative activities was legion; their only reward was satisfaction in knowing the society could install a heating system or paint one side of the building.

"Time for my cigar, Carrie."

## Gates and Bars

The society's Historic Sites Committee was formed to develop a series of educational and recreational tours of locations within the town boundaries. Tours were free to members - a payback of sorts.

The first outing was an easy walk around the center of town to learn the history and origin of each building that ringed the common, which now, thirty years later, is on the National Register of Historic Places.

Our second tour was more ambitious for both the leaders and the participants. Billed as a visit to early town cemeteries, the deeper we got into the planning, the clearer it became we would need four-wheel drive vehicles to traverse roads classified by the town as "Closed - Subject to Gates and Bars". This New Hampshire jargon translated into "proceed at your own risk; if your vehicle gets stuck, we're not pulling you out".

Pickup trucks, the only vehicles at the time equipped with four-wheel drive traction, were pressed into service to accommodate the roads and the fifty society members who clamored to be included. When tour day arrived, we piled the truck beds with hay and loaded in our passengers with the help of a stepstool.

The excitement and enthusiasm of the group was overwhelming as they climbed on board. I was acutely aware of our responsibility as I counted heads and realized fifty percent of them were either white or gray. An awe-inspiring testimony to ignoring one's age in the face of what one really wants to do.

We tossed and bounced over rutted, overgrown roads left to decay as centers of towns were relocated and boundaries redefined. Age did show its true colors as bladders reacted to the rough ride. The single roll of toilet tissue I had brought for emergencies, dwindled to a precious few sheets as it was passed from hand-to-hand. It soon became clear it was not solely for history's sake my elderly companions dashed into the Revolutionary War Cemetery seeking out some of the *larger* monuments. The tour was an enormous success.

## Night Crawlers

Kay spent every summer in Fitzwilliam following her first visit to my cabin. It was natural that she caught my love for the town and its heritage. I wasted no time snapping her up for duty on the Historic Sites Committee. A tireless worker and superlative organizer, very quickly she became embroiled in planning and preparing for upcoming tours.

Side-by-side at the famous Webb granite quarry, we used sickles, clippers, and weed-wackers to clear pathways and undergrowth to enhance the view of Mt. Monadnock. We tied yellow caution tape from tree-to-tree on the perimeter of the quarry to keep people from getting too near the edge. When granite faded in popularity for building construction, the quarry filled with water and became an enticing but unsafe swimming spot. It was even rumored its limitless depth was the last resting place for a few junk cars.

We were completely unprepared for the graffiti on the facing wall of the quarry. I stared at it in disbelief. "What a dreadful view for the tour group," I said. "If only there was a way to keep them from seeing that. We have to think of something."

Kay looked around from where she was tying her end of the yellow tape and said, "Please don't suggest we walk all the way around to the other side and lower a tarp to cover a bunch of four-letter words. That's out."

I'd forgotten "pragmatic" was her middle name until she continued, "These people know what kids can do. Most of the tour group are older than you and won't be as shocked as you are. Age doesn't wear blinders and old doesn't mean you stay home and let the world run by itself. Some of the most passionate people I know are in their eighties. Leave it. There's nothing you can do." Of course she was right.

We numbered the tour sites with small signs that corresponded with maps and literature the participants would carry as they walked the route. We had learned the hard way never to trust New Hampshire weather and waited until the wee hours of tour day to put up these numbers. Armed with flashlights, we crept along dirt roads on foot, in and out of cellar holes, through woods and over stone walls. There was no fear we'd disturb anyone because the places were long since deserted by the original inhabitants. Now, one hundred years later, we only startled an owl or two, a couple of stray cats and a mother fox whose shiny eyes stared angrily from her den. Her kits mewed in frustration at having their meal interrupted by two night-crawling old ladies.

Back to Butts

It followed that, along with me, Kay volunteered to take charge of the Sanitation Committee for the upcoming Antiques Show. Our leader told us use of the town hall bathroom facilities was no longer permitted. Fifty-five antique dealers would set up booths on the town common attracting crowds of lookers and buyers. Potential traffic in and out of the c. 1800 town hall to use the ancient plumbing/septic system resulted in the selectmen's decision to close the building to the public.

Porta-Potties to the rescue. Porta-Potties, those bright blue or green metal huts trucked over the road to crowd-gathering events by enterprising vendors who trafficked in human waste. They were true spinners of dross into gold, the very essence of alchemy. Still, PP's were a shamefully welcome sight if you were in need. It turned out almost every man, woman and child who passed through town was in need that day. After all, one couldn't miss the telltale huts sticking out in full view on the side lawn of the historic town hall.

Our instructions had read: "Bring card table, liquid soap, basin of water and paper towels for those stepping out of the PP's to wash and dry their hands, also extra rolls of toilet tissue. Cruise the area every half hour to be sure all is tidy and replenished." The latch on one of the potty doors was missing. A typical ingenious Yankee, Kay fashioned a hook using a chain of woven twisties. This was added to our list of checkpoints.

I should have had immense pride in the magnitude of the responsibility we had been given. Instead, appalled, I said to Kay, "I had no idea this was going to mushroom into an all-day task."

Were we humbled by this chore? You bet. Again we had ignored our ages and blundered into a task which would never be a feature article in AARP's *Modern Maturity*. What could have been a fairly acceptable job on a day in spring or fall turned into a strenuous effort, not one for the faint of heart. The heat consumed us as well as every last bit of the deodorizer cakes in the PP's. As each user entered these bake ovens, I worried that as they relieved themselves, they would fry in mid-bliss. The heat intensified through the day and the huts' aluminum sides groaned louder with each opening and closing of the doors. An inadvertent bump against them sent out a thunderous reverberation across the center of town.

Why was I doing this, I asked myself? Weren't the cigarette butts enough of a lesson? Was I afraid of getting stalled on a treadmill where the elderly often found themselves? No. It wasn't fear. It was ignorance. Too dumb to consider my age when I should be taking it into account, and too smart to spend my days living off memories, smelling of lavender and sipping cambric tea.

"Wouldn't you think," I asked Kay, who was on her knees in front of the blue Porta-Potty affixing a new hook of twisties, "it would be embarrassing to those half our age sitting over there under umbrellas taking money and handing out tickets when they see us out here in the hot sun doing this menial job?"

She looked over her shoulder at me and said, "Stop worrying what people think and get more toilet paper."

Suddenly I thought, did I tell her we still had to pick up cigarette butts on the common? I wondered if I'd be able to bend over after this hellish day with the hoppers. I jumped as she called out, "Keep moving. You'll age quicker standing still."

I wanted Kay to be a visible and viable part of my life from the start of our relationship. Therefore it was important to bring her into my involvements as much as possible and to the extent she would allow. Shy around people, she was most comfortable behind-the-scenes. "I'm a poor chief, but I make a great Indian," she told me.

I was envious of how introspective she was; how readily she knew where she belonged and therefore was able to make great contributions. I am a risk-taker and I think with my heart. Before I met her this often landed me in places I shouldn't have been. From her I began to recognize what's important and what isn't; it's a great lesson learned. Some people belong on the stage, others should work behind it.

Everyone is important. Kay is a perfect example of this.

# THE SPLENDOR OF SHEETROCK AND SHIPLAP

*"...the question is not how old you are, but how you are old..."*
Art Linkletter

## A Rainy Day

It was a boring Tuesday in mid-July. Rain had us stuck inside the cabin where we did not want to be; ripe blueberries waited to be picked and gardens needed cultivating.

Because of the rain, we lingered over breakfast. Lingering was a luxury for some, but morning was the best part of our day. It was one of the first things we had learned about each other: we were both morning people.

Ordinarily by 6 a.m. we had walked West Lake Road for two miles. Then, back on the deck, we'd watch the sun come up over the lake. The sun played games as it rose behind the trees. It sparkled now here, now there; until finally bursting free, its brilliance momentarily blinded us. Great shafts fell from the sky leaving a glow on everything they touched. On Sundays it was a ritual to take our breakfast champagne on the deck and toast the magnificence of God's work spread before us.

The musky odor of damp earth, of things rotting and dying, filled the early morning air. I had carved out a small space for the cabin in dense woods; centuries of forest bottom had awakened like a sleeping giant. As the sun circled the house during the day, heat replaced the damp odors of morning with the smell of sweet fern and pine that swirled in the air like an exploding spice rack.

By evening the sun dropped behind the cabin in the western sky. As its eyes closed for the day, there was a brief moment when the the eastern treetops were tipped with a golden finger of warm frosting. The damp smells of the morning gradually returned as darkness fell.

45

Suddenly Kay sat forward in her chair flapping a newspaper circular. "Here's what we should do today."

Because it was something we loved to do on rainy days I guessed, "Antiquing?"

"No," she said giving the paper a more urgent shake, "purchase some of these wall panels. See? They're on sale in Keene. We can do the bathroom and get rid of the damned Percale in that room."

With that simple statement life at the cabin was turned upside down for the next three years.

## Deciding Who's Boss

Kay had always wanted to work with her hands as well as her brain and had taken a course on "Carpentry for Women". A perfectionist, she became an accomplished carpenter.

I can still see the official carpenter's belt she wore at "quick draw" level. It holstered screwdrivers, pliers and nails plus the business-like hammer that bounced against her thigh and boasted, "A nail head with every blow!"

Her first summer at the cabin, Kay tackled the bathroom sink where for five years I had balanced a cake of soap, toothbrushes and toothpaste around the porcelain edges; other lotions and potions were lined up on the floor. Her magic resulted in plenty of counter space for a soap dish and a state-of-the-art toothbrush and paste holder. The new shelf beneath the sink was instantly pressed into service for cleaning supplies. Antique barn boards strung together with knotted clothesline became a unique set of hanging shelves. Here I placed my best looking bottles of lotion and even found room for a vase of dried flowers. What a clever person my "Avon Lady" turned out to be.

Then along came this rainy day and the newspaper circular with an ad for paneling. The antique blue color would be perfect in my rustic little house.

In the afternoon we returned from Keene with five handsome knotty pine panels carefully loaded into the station wagon by the helpful hardware person. It now fell to Kay and me to transport the panels through the rain, up the steps and into the house. It was a short portage and looked doable...but five times?

Although I wasn't intimidated by the task, the memory of the first time we attempted to synchronize our efforts came to mind immediately. I said nothing but smiled to myself as I mentally replayed that event. Kay had brought her canoe to the lake and kept it on the shore at my waterfront. She took it out regularly by herself, but I shied away from going because, city girl that I was, my water experience was limited. However Kay, the professional water safety instructor, possessed more knowledge than anyone would ever need to know about paddling a canoe. On the day of my first excursion, she settled in the stern and graciously steadied the wobbly craft for me to get in the bow. I decided to keep to myself that I had never been in a canoe before. I just knew she would think, why would she own access to the lake if she didn't know how to use it? It was somehow important for me to show her that I wasn't a complete dope. Once seated, I grabbed my paddle and worked furiously to help get us away from the dock. After a few seconds of flapping arms and paddle like an out-of-control windmill, I realized we hadn't moved at all - we were dead in the water. It took only a quick glance at Kay's exaggerated expression of tolerance to guess what she was thinking - over sixty and hasn't learned to paddle a canoe. I burst out laughing as I realized I was *facing* her and of course we were at a stalemate. Stoically, she re-steadied the canoe while I turned around.

Now here we were with a really important job to do together. The panels were awkward and heavy. Nevertheless, carrying them horizontally with one at each end, we started off walking forward side-by-side. The path soon became too narrow and we had to change positions midway. After shouting directions at one another, we started up once more. The path was full of rocks and roots which made the going slow. By the time we reached the steps leading up to the front door, our hands were sore and we each blamed the other for our difficulties.

"You should have placed your hands like I have mine."

"Why do you have to go so damned fast?"

"It's raining or are you so dense you can't feel it?"

The arguments intensified as we planned our ascent. We barked orders back and forth.

"Mind you don't drag *your* end in the mud."

"Mind you don't nick *your* end on the roof overhang."

Kay finally made it to the top of the steps. "Oh, God, she groaned, "the screen door opens *out!*" We were forced to back down and get the door open before we could regroup, issue each other new sets of orders and press on. By the time we had the fifth panel through the door, we were moving more efficiently and certainly more silently; we were too exhausted to speak.

It is said ignorance is bliss and in our case it surely was. It was

The arguments intensified

also a test of our friendship. We had said things to one another that would have driven two younger women apart, but we had mellowed with age and most of the time knew where our priorities were. Perhaps the biggest blessing was that we had started off small. Kay had energy to burn, her skill was unfailing, and by the end of the week she had paneled the entire bathroom. We had walls.

Over the rest of the summer we insulated all the outer walls and for sound buffers, some interior ones too. Like two ants with a rubber tree plant, we carried the huge rolls of pink insulation into the house. The stuff was loaded with minute particles of fiber glass. Whenever we handled it Kay covered every exposed part of her, even to a white plastic face mask over her nose and mouth. I had all I could do to keep from "ha-ha-ing" out loud at the sight of my gray-haired friend wearing the conical mask, work hat down over her eyes and ears; shirt buttoned to her chin. She could have been preparing to wield a pickaxe in a Welsh coal mine rather than a staple gun in a cabin in the New Hampshire woods.

## The Turn of the Worm

The early days of our shared lives have so many wonderful memories that, as I contemplated writing this memoir, I had to catalog and categorize those memories. I created a series of portfolios from that library in my mind. One memory led to another and soon they were coming so fast I couldn't believe my seventy-year old mentality was in such good working order.

The winter following the destruction of hardwood trees by gypsy moth caterpillars, we read that the same insulation we'd installed in the house, when put up pink side out, and laced with petroleum jelly, was an effective shield with which to wrap trees. The caterpillars' jellied feet would become trapped in the fuzzy maze of fiber glass. We decided to make an early spring trip to the lake and get the jump on the worms by wrapping the hardwoods closest to the house with our leftover insulation.

Spring was close at hand in Durham, but Fitzwilliam's much higher altitude still had knee-deep snow. Because of this we were unable to park close to the cabin and donned the snowshoes that always rode with us in winter. Kay managed buckles and straps smoothly, balancing and kneeling with grace and agility. Once shod, she stood and watched me labor into mine. I was not agile and my knees never cooperated when I really needed them. I was forced to bend from the hips

49

to insert my boot into the snowshoe strap. I could always count on falling over at least once.

Kay got busy measuring the circumference of the trees while I headed for the cabin to get the insulation, jelly, scissors and staple gun. Faced with having to remove the snowshoes, I made an instant decision to leave them on. There were only eight steps leading up to the front door, but they were quite steep. To me, it was the lesser of two evils. Like a clown in oversized shoes, I threaded my awkward feet onto the stair treads. It took me so long, my partner trotted around the corner of the house to find me and discovered I was wedged halfway up the flight, with a huge foot stuck on two separate stairs. I teetered dangerously and would have snapped off my legs at the ankles had I tipped backwards,

"What were you thinking?"

"Anything was better than taking these off."

Once free I still refused to shed the snowshoes and clomped into the house to get the supplies. To retrace my route, I sat on the top step and inched my way down.

Any gypsy moths who watched our efforts from their winter nests were surely strategizing their onslaught. However, that was not the case. Could the sight of oak trees decorated in fuzzy pink have taken away their appetites? Whatever the reason, the slithering hordes of worms passed over us that year. We knew if we hadn't defended the trees, the worms would not have turned.

Laying Hot Bricks

Kay's skill at paneling the bathroom led us to discuss the possibility of the cabin becoming a year-round home. The only source of heat presently in the house was the small electric baseboard heating units. Electricity costs had skyrocketed, limiting the luxury of heat to the bathroom.

We drove to Peterborough and looked at Vermont Castings woodstoves. It was hard for me to believe that such attractive fixtures could be functional. We decided on a bright red Intrepid, the smallest size. The beauty of these stoves is the duality of their operation, either as an open fireplace or a slow burning woodstove. The salesman stressed the importance of having solid insulation under and behind the stove to protect the walls from the intense heat radiating from stove and chimney pipe.

Jimmy Geoffries lived in town and was known for beautiful

workmanship in a variety of media - wood, stone and brick. He had a reputation for other things as well. A silver-tongued user of women, he first wormed his way into their good graces and then mooched off them. A divorcée named Suzy was his current assignation although I'd heard rumors about a rift in their relationship.

Jimmy looked at the stove area and suggested a brick hearth leading to a brick wall. He spoke of some used brick he had that would be perfect for the job.

"Only one problem. I can't do the job myself. My brother, George, is an excellent mason and I'll come over and see how the work progresses." Disapppointed as I was, the hearth needed to be completed before the stove could be delivered and I agreed.

George arrived the next morning driving a pickup loaded with classic used brick. He went right to work and by noon the hearth was done. When he returned from his break and began the courses of brick for the back wall, it was obvious he'd had a liquid lunch. He stumbled over his own feet and everything in his path. He struggled to keep from falling down as he came in with armloads of brick.

Kay gestured at George's work and mouthed, "Look what he's done."

The wall was totally askew. In fact, it leaned toward the kitchen at a ridiculous slant. When Jimmy arrived to inspect the work, he ordered his brother off the job. The next morning Jimmy himself returned, took down the crooked wall, replaced it and put in a handsome piece of beautifully stained and polished pine for a mantlepiece. I paid him the minute the last brick was in place and waved him off; a few leftover bricks bounced along in the back of the pickup.

Within two hours Suzy phoned. After some small talk she asked, "Do you have a hearth of used brick in your house?" When I said I did she went on, "Those are my bricks, you know."

"No, Suzy. They're mine. I paid for them just this morning when Jimmy finished the job."

"Well, he stole them from me and I want them back. He moved out yesterday. Just cleaned out his stuff and took off. Then I noticed the pile of brick was gone too."

I told her I was sorry for her trouble and added, "But the bricks aren't leaving my house."

When I hung up the phone I said to Kay, "I wonder who the mantlepiece belonged to?"

We laughed over the events of the last two days. I know she

51

felt the same as I did; we were fortunate, cherished our independence and did not need the attention of the Jimmy Geoffries of the world. I respected myself too much anyway.

## Forty-five Degrees of Shiplap

The living room with its vaulted cathedral ceiling was the focal point of the cabin. A sliding glass door led to the deck and, along with a tall narrow triple window, took up half of one wall. The hearth and brick insulation for the woodstove covered the back of the room. We had insulated this area the year before and were tired of reading the manufacturer's advertising that repeated itself over and over on the facing paper.

It was back to hardware headquarters to study more panels. None looked "right" for the room in which we did all our living until we saw the shiplap. These tongue-and-groove boards were new to us and were an intriguing concept because they offered a rough and a smooth side. It was natural wood, could be stained or allowed to darken at its own pace. We were sold.

Kay's idea for cutting and fitting the shiplap at a 45 degree angle was a tribute to her mathematical genius and design capabilities. By dividing the dimensions of the longest wall in two, she designed mirror images of the configuration that reduced the calculations to manageable size and created a remarkable wall mosaic. Given the 45 degree ingredient, even her intricate mind could not come up with the exact quantity of shiplap required for the entire room. The first delivery of the lumber looked mountainous and threatening when it was stacked on the deck. Two sawhorses joined the party on the deck and the games began.

Let it be noted that every piece of shiplap Kay installed was individually measured, sawed and sanded by hand. We chose to have the more rustic, rough side face the room. Easy enough, you say? With each piece measured and cut, she also had to remember which side of the board was to be "out". On the few times she had a "senior moment" in these procedures and the 45 degree angle pointed the wrong way, she'd have to begin again. Her Yankee frugality surfaced at such times and all but a few wrong-angle mistakes were fitted in elsewhere in the room.

The job took two years to complete but when finished, it became a topic of conversation. Everyone who entered the house for the first time was in awe. Not just by the skill, both creative and mathematical, but by what could be done by a sixty-year old woman.

In those days Kay was fresh from the feminist movement and barely acknowledged compliments that were tied to her gender. Anyway, her projects had just begun.

Swing Time

My house was positioned on a knoll. The land fell away from that point and the dirt roadway was steep as it descended to the water. This was a short post-lunch walk and it revved us up for the tasks that lay ahead. Plus the aerobic exercise of the eighth-mile trek back up the hill brought an insurgence of wonderful air into our lungs, to say nothing of the benefit to muscle tone and heart rate. All of this provided our sexagesimal systems with more benefits than any vitamins could offer.

Another favorite walk was down West Lake Road to the public beach. This was beneficial in many ways: there might be ripe blueberries to pick along the way and here was the best view of Mt. Monadnock as it looked down on Laurel Lake. In early morning hours, when cool air met warm lake water, mist hung like misguided clouds framing the distant peak. The rising sun slowly made its approach until finally it glanced off the side of the mountain. Kilimanjaro could not have looked more majestic.

On one of these walks Kay spotted something shiny resting at the sandy bottom of the crystal clear water five yards from shore.

"Looks like a quarter," she said and pointed at something lost to my trifocals. "Think I'll wade in and get it." She removed her shoes and rolled up her jeans. As I watched her step into the cold water I thought, is this what being a Yankee is all about? Pennsylvania native that I was, I would never have considered wading into the cold lake at six in the morning - unless it was a sure thing.

Kay was determined. When she reached her quarry she called back, "It *is* a quarter and there's more further out." Already wet up to her crotch and up one arm, she pushed on through the water. The total "take from the lake" was $1.25.

"Was it worth it?" I asked her as she slogged her way home.

"Of course. I'll treat myself to a sundae with it."

Years have passed since our time at the lake but we still take long walks every day. We seem to have always known the benefits of walking. Today the term "swing time" is used to define the period one's foot spends off the ground when walking. Studies show old people

53

develop very short swing times if they don't walk regularly. Some in their sixties even shuffle just to keep their balance. Swing time meant something totally different in my day.

Martha's Place

I lost count long ago of the number of times people came into the cabin and said, "Oh! Your kitchen is *so* different."

One comment I never heard was, "How do you ever work in here?" If anyone *had* asked me, I'm not sure I would have been able to give an intelligent answer. I was so used to it I could stand in the middle of the floor and reach everything I needed in one grand pivot.

Orange crates and narrow wooden bureau drawers hung sideways from the open studs where they served as shelves for everyday glasses and mugs. An 1890's wooden tray stand, a relic from the inn, held a toaster oven, boxes of cereal, rice and pasta along with canned goods including mega-amounts of cat and dog food. Pots and pans hung from ceiling beams. Pottery jars, balanced on the mini-counter around the sink, held silverware and cooking utensils. An array of mismatched canisters stood on a small drop-leaf table. These contained the usual flour, sugar, tea bags and dog biscuits.

A large chicken-feed bin that came out of the barn I had owned in the village served as storage for dishes, a counter for eating and a place to set up board and card games. We had to sit on high stools to reach the surface. Unfortunately, our knees butted up against the bin and made it hard to get close to a plate of food.

The pièce de résistance, and one of the few kitchen accouterments to survive the remodeling, was an antique ladder hung horizontally on the wall next to the kitchen. It was the focal point of the room and held my collection of brightly colored cocktail glasses.

Despite its unique qualities and arrangement of kitchen utensils, working and cooking in the kitchen was close to impossible. There were no cupboards, and the lack of counter space meant nothing could be left out for even a moment lest it fall to the floor or plunge into the sink. Kay was intrigued by the architectural challenges the cubicle presented. She turned her attention to its improvement as soon as she had "shiplapped" her way around to the kitchen. In just one summer she converted a sow's ear into a Martha Stewart icon complete with shelves and counter space. Cupboards were fashioned from old bookcases to which she attached her handcrafted lattice-work doors.

Rather than continue the shiplap pattern into the kitchen, we decided to put up sheetrock and hang wallpaper. It sounded easy, something I could help with where my limited talent wouldn't get in the way. I blithely asked, "How much sheetrock would we need?"

As we stood looking around the kitchen, Kay said, "About four sheets. The stuff is a pretty big deal just to measure and cut. Just getting it onto the sawhorses and in and out of the kitchen to make size adjustments won't be easy."

"I'll help you," I said. Kay rolled her eyes and I just knew she pictured me on the other end of a 4 x 8 sheet of drywall. I found out sheetrock weighed three times as much as the bathroom panels. I knew I was in trouble when I dropped my end of the first sheet we carried and snapped off a corner. I put my knee through the next when I tripped over a root.

Kay persevered undaunted until she had walled in the entire kitchen, but we contracted out the drywall work in the rest of the rooms.

Two for the Scaffold

The vast cathedral ceiling in the living room remained unfinished. We hadn't insulated this area because it was impossible for us to reach. I fretted over the expensive electric heat that escaped through the roof in spring and fall when the woodstove by itself couldn't cut the cold. We knew the ceiling work was a definite two-person undertaking, but discarded the idea of using step ladders with a plank across as being too tricky; anyway none of the ladders we had were tall enough. I'm not sure who said it first, but suddenly the word "scaffolding" was loose in the air.

"Scaffolding," I said, rolling the word over my tongue. "That's the contraption workers put up when they paint up high or brick a wall." Kay nodded in agreement.

"That's heavy wooden planks laid across an iron frame on wheels. How could we ever assemble it?"

"We could. First we'd need a truck to bring it from the rental place; actually we could rent the truck too. We could do the insulation in two days and the whole job wouldn't cost much."

A rush of memories brings back the scene as we pulled up to the Taylor Rent-All the next day. We drove a bright red pickup truck and the two male clerks lounging in the doorway watched our approach. Their attitude dripped with tongue-in-cheek machoism as they waited to see who the two "dolls" in the flashy GMC turned out to be. They

"We need a third person"

waited and watched as Kay swung the truck around, backed it up to the entrance with all the finesse of an eighteen-wheel driver with "first seat" credentials.

We announced we had come to pick up the scaffolding we'd reserved by telephone. Stunned, the clerks looked at each other. As if we had spoken in Swahili, one of them said, "*You're* here for the scaffolding?"

Vastly amused, the second clerk looked us both up and down and asked, "Watcha gonna do with it?" Obviously we were not young, but that wasn't what confounded him; it was the fact we were women.

"Ceiling work," Kay answered.

"Your husbands send you?"

"Do you have to have one of those to use a scaffold?"

"No, ma'am; but it sure would make it easier."

Kay, short on patience when it came to being slotted into a steretypical female role, said, "Just point us to the scaffold and we'll be out of here."

Neither of us had ever seen a scaffold up close before; broken down, *never.* Nor did we have any idea how much the sections weighed. However, we tacitly decided this was not the time or place to ask too many questions. When we saw there were only two pieces and they were on wheels, we stole ecstatic looks at each other. We pushed the sections to the truck and heaved them aboard through the tailgate. The two clerks brought up the rear carrying the three flooring planks.

We had already moved all the furniture to one end of the living room and there was ample space to maneuver once we had the sections inside the house. The trick now was for each of us to hold up one piece of scaffolding, the proper distance from the other, and then snap the metal connecting bars into slots that would hold the rig together.

Every time I reached out to grab the connector bar from Kay, the wheels took over and the sections went flying, pulling us both with them.

"We need a third person," I said.

"We don't have one."

"I'm tired of this thing falling on me."

"Try holding your tongue differently."

We loaded our precut insulation onto the scaffolding along with the staple gun and Kay's mask. Then we climbed on board. Because I suffered from vertigo, I couldn't look down from where we stood twelve feet off the floor. Working over my head all the time wasn't easy either; I often had to grab for the scaffold rail to keep from pitching off. We were amazed at how quickly and smoothly the job went; we were half done by early afternoon.

"We should consider putting up the ceiling panels tomorrow while we still have the truck and the scaffold," Kay proposed. "We don't want to deal with this contraption - or those two birds at the rent-all - ever again in our lives."

"How many panels this time?" I couldn't believe she was serious.

When Kay said, "About twenty-five should do it," I cringed behind my eyelids as I visualized our last experience. The idea that we would haul all of these to the house and install over half of them in one day seemed insurmountable, but we plowed ahead.

The building supply store opened at 7 a.m. even on Sunday and we got started while our energy was still at peak level. We milled around in the lumber shed and rubbed shoulders with the weekend carpenters. We were the only women but were included in the spontaneous comraderie that seemed to go with the anticipation of building something by hand. We were accepted even though our gender, wrinkles and gray hair stood out in the crowd.

Our antique body parts were faced with the ultimate challenge as we began the enormous task we had set for ourselves. Each panel was raised over our heads and jockeyed into position. While I held my end in place, Kay nailed her end to the ceiling studs; then I nailed mine. In order to see where to place the paneling nails, we had to lean backwards at an 80 degree angle. From the discomfort of this awkward stance, driving in the nails took tremendous effort. Each hammer blow sent shudders rocketing from elbows to wrists. We constantly had to massage our upper arms to restore feeling and get the blood flowing down into our hands and fingers. It was back-breaking work and we amazed ourselves as each panel was secured.

As we worked my mind rushed ahead to our evening happy hour and I said, "Have you thought how good our wine's going to taste?"

"When we get to it."

We disassembled the scaffold, loaded it into the truck and returned both to Keene. Back at the cabin, we raised our wine glasses to the paneling job that soared over our heads.

"I wonder if anyone will believe we did the ceiling ourselves?"

I asked.

"Only if it falls down."

## Life in the Batting

When we returned to the cabin the next spring, we thought the nightly chorus of squeaks we heard was coming from outside. Then we wondered if something was living a secret life in the insulation we'd so carefully stapled into the cathedral ceiling. The question was answered the evening we were privy to the first flying lesson of six tiny bats. From out of nowhere the lofty air space above our heads was filled with swooping, chattering shapes. With bodies hardly bigger than humming birds, their oversized wings allowed the babies to perform extraordinary aerial acrobatics seemingly far beyond their age. Obviously the coach, a larger bat clung to the edge of the topmost panel. As unexpectedly as they appeared, the entire flock faded back into the ceiling.

The exterminator made the mistake of telling us he'd have to tear out all the panels and insulation to be sure he could reach and destroy all the bats. We knew we'd never allow him to rip out our work. We also knew the bats were harmless, ate certain antisocial bugs and would probably move on once the babies were out of the nest. The exterminator wasn't encouraging at all, but our minds were made up and we continued to live side-by-side with the tiny mammals for years.

## Good-bye

I'm not sure which caught up with me first: the taxes on my waterfront or the recognition that as much as I tried to ignore it, I was too old to live in such an isolated place full of accidents waiting to happen.

We did most of the outside work ourselves which involved keeping the property free of undergrowth, cutting firewood, maintaining the footpath from house to lake and raking the entire length of the dirt roads. We hired contractors for unplanned maintenance jobs such as shoring up the house when it began to sag, or freeing the sewer pipe from the clutches of tree roots which prevented the smooth flow of waste to the septic tank.

The final wake-up call came when I broke my ankle in a dispute with a rock that had been in the yard longer than I had. Immobilized by a knee-high plaster cast, I was forced to sit and watch Kay shoulder the full load of house and yard work along with my care and feeding. I felt every minute of my age. The full connotation of the word "old" loomed on the horizon. I saw what the future held if I didn't take action, so I did.

It was a bittersweet moment when we said good-bye to our simple life in the woods. Kay and I had shared the cabin for sixteen years; I had owned it for twenty-five. The cabin will always emerge as one of the greatest achievements in my life.

To age is one thing - to feel old is another. It was time to move on.

## Reflections

On two occasions, in other times and places, I had exchanged vows "to love and honor...in sickness and in health". No such spoken pledge ever existed between Kay and me and yet, whenever the darkness of crisis descends, we reach out to each other with unselfish concern. We have each said, "My life is upside down when things aren't right in yours."

Some years ago, Kay fell from the roof of our house when the ladder slid out from under her. After calling 911 and covering her with a blanket, I knelt beside her on the ground and began to pray. As I prayed it was revealed to me the very breadth of all she had come to mean to me. "I know she's an aging lady, but don't let her die. We have so much more to do."

Kay prayed similarly when I had food poisoning so deadly I lost consciousness and ended up in the emergency room.

We listen more and more to the crones within. Wisely, they have shed light on the importance of compassionate coping "in sickness and in health".

# GETTING HOME IS THE BEST PART

*"...nothing brings back childhood memories like the whistle of a train..."*
MLF

## "Caught Between the Moon and New York City"

All eyes were on me as reverberations from the gas-propelled cork ricochetted around one of Logan airport's small coffee shops; the sound bounced from tiled ceiling to cement floor. Ordinarily unflappable business travelers were rattled out of their morning newspapers into startled consciousness. Security guards were on the alert and began to move in our direction.

It was 7 a.m. Two friends had come to Boston to see me off on a trip to Las Vegas I'd dreamed about for a year. They knew my "white knuckle" approach to flying and decided to force-feed me champagne to make my takeoff easier and more fluid. We were seated at the cafe table when they produced a magnum of Taylor's best.

I was traveling alone on my way to the desert southwest for a camping trip with people from Fitzwilliam. As the day of departure drew closer, my terror of being trapped thousands of miles in the air escalated. Just thinking about being locked in the airtight craft released claustrophobic symptoms over which I had no control.

Prepared to literally pour me onto the plane, once the cork was popped they handed me the first of several glasses. Embarrassed by my need for a champagne crutch to board the flight, I nodded to the applauding onlookers and tossed back the bubbly in a single swallow. By the time we were over Chicago, I *was* flying; quite independent of the plane.

I can count on the fingers of one hand the times I have set foot on an airplane. In those few flights I endured an aborted takeoff, which ended in a nose-stand at the end of the runway, and a landing at a small rural airport in a fierce thunder and lightning storm where,

61

blinded by tears of relief, I got to my knees and kissed the ground.

The *coup de grâce* was a night landing in New York. Socked in by fog, incoming planes to Kennedy Airport were allowed to land only as visibility permitted; which wasn't often. Thousands of feet above New York, moonlight shone brightly. Out the window I counted twenty planes below ours each circling in its own holding pattern. With trepidation I wondered how many that I couldn't see were stacked up overhead. It would take just one wrong altimeter reading to bring us all crashing to the ground.

My fellow passengers included a newlywed couple headed for a connecting flight and a Bermuda honeymoon. Still in her white gown and veil, in full voice the bride wailed over spoiled plans. She berated the tuxedo-clad groom with cutting remarks about booking last minute flights and how he should have known better. Migrant farm workers bound for home, excitedly shouted back and forth in their native tongue. Their cries of consternation rose to an earsplitting crescendo.

Like a line from the movie *Arthur*, we were "caught between the moon and New York City".

Making Tracks

I made a pact with myself that, except for a life-and-death emergency, I would never fly again. To date I've been able to honor that decision. Kay, understanding friend that she is, never attempted to dissuade me with statistical arguments in favor of air travel. She knew safety wasn't the issue; it was my need to get off the plane the moment it was pressurized and taxiing to the runway.

The year Josh couldn't get home for Christmas, we decided to take the holiday to him in Ft. Lauderdale. Along with Amey we left Boston's South Station just before New Year's. Seat reservations were required on Amtrak's Silver Streak out of New York, but not on the five-hour northeast corridor run from Boston. We were overwhelmed by the crowds of people in the station and the stampede for seats once the barrier was lowered at the boarding gate. Our suitcases banged against our legs as we raced down the platform to the coaches. I was also encumbered by a three-foot teddy bear I was determined to deliver to Josh in person.

The bulk of our thirty-six hour journey was the leg from New York to Ft. Lauderdale. It seemed simple enough to sit up all night as we planned the trip in our New Hampshire living room. What we couldn't adequately picture was how close the train coach would come

I had to share my seat with a three-foot teddy bear

to a sardine's environment. By the end of the first day I had yet to figure out what to do with my legs and feet and still faced the long night sitting up in my seat. Already I dreaded the return trip.

My first impression of Ft. Lauderdale was white highrise buildings, causeways and soaring drawbridges surrounded by a network of canals, rivers, bays and inlets. There were flashy "cigarette" boats tied up at docks behind spacious waterfront residences.

"Boats outnumber the cars. There must be three to a family," I said in amazement.

We were staying in a canal-side timeshare condo. The owner, a client of Josh's, was away for the week and magically the place was ours.

It was unseasonably cold in Ft. Lauderdale that year. Accompanied by a biting wind, it made the three miles of gorgeous beaches off-limits. The hours I spent in a Dover, New Hampshire, tanning salon provided the tan I was destined not to get in Florida. The closest we got to the water was the warm jacuzzi that came with our condo. "Breezy resort wear" was suggested by the Florida tour book but we stayed bundled up in the sweaters and windbreakers we had worn leaving New Hampshire.

Despite the weather, we enjoyed a Water Taxi tour of the Intracoastal Waterways. Josh joined us for dinner at the famous Chart House restaurant; afterwards we crossed over the bay by boat to a stage show at the Broward Center for the Performing Arts.

Jonah Escapes Poseidon

It was a true test of our adaptibility to come from rural New Hampshire to the energetic sophistication of Ft. Lauderdale, a city known as much for its resort-hopping wealthy as its teenage spring break revelers. Las Olas Boulevard overflowed with expensive shoppes which we carefully avoided in favor of Burdine's Department Store where Josh worked as a hair designer.

It was in the travel agency next door that he saw brochures advertising a one-day cruise to the Bahamas. We decided the cruise would be a great way to greet the New Year and locked ourselves into a voyage so horrifying it became our very own *Poseidon Adventure*. We booked passage for five which included Josh and his friend, Bill Kelly, who had never been to sea before. Ever.

Sea Escape, or "Escape from the Sea" as we call it to this day, would take us to Freeport in the Bahamas and back for $99 per person.

Included in the price was round-trip bus fare to the Port of Miami, buffet breakfast served on board and a dinner buffet on the return trip. Staterooms could be reserved for an extra cost on a first-come, first-served basis. The booking agent explained that, while the ship could comfortably handle a large number on a one-day outing, overnight accommodations were available for only a few passengers. In a nutshell, there were not enough staterooms to go around for all who wanted one. We had booked early and therefore had a private bathroom as well as a place to change into bathing suits.

"I wonder why this cruise is so cheap?" I asked Josh.

"Gambling starts the minute the boat is in international waters," he answered. "The games are probably rigged in favor of Sea Escape."

The morning of our trip was perfect Florida weather. The blue Atlantic mirrored the color of the sky and the sun created golden windows in the buildings along the Miami coastline.

We made our way up to the pool deck as soon as we boarded. Here vividly colored chairs ranged across the deck like a spilled bag of M&M's. Just off the pool deck was the cocktail lounge. The bar was at one end where brightly labeled liquor bottles were flanked on either side by rows of waiting cocktail glasses of every size and shape. The room fanned out to the full width of the ship where there were tables and wicker armchairs. The seat cushions were covered in tropical-print fabrics. It was a comfortable room and we looked forward to a pre-dinner drink on the return trip.

Through the lounge was the dining room; gleaming stainless steel buffet counters took up the center area. Stacks of white china plates stood in readiness at one end. The steam table gave off a delicious aroma which forecast the breakfast delights advertised as "all you can eat". We found seats at one of the tables which were chained to anchor locks in the floor. None of us could imagine the need for such extreme measures: the ocean was like a pond.

Breakfast was a feast of fruit, eggs, potatoes, three kinds of meat, biscuits and gravy, French toast, pancakes and an assortment of muffins, breads and Danish pastries.

We made our way back to the pool deck after we had eaten. As we stepped outside Kay said, "It's raining. What happened to our beautiful day?"

"Jonah on board," I jokingly replied never realizing how close to Jonah's fate we were to come.

Streaks of lightning shot through the darkening sky. The sea became rougher as ground swells increased in size. Thunder crashed all around. Except for the gamblers already gathered in the game room, everyone moved down the companion ways to the lower deck. Those that had staterooms headed for them, including Josh and Bill. Instinct told me that below the water line was the wrong place to be on a rolling sea and I went after them.

As I went down the stairs, passengers who had no staterooms were lined up in the passageways. Overcome by seasickness, first one and then another, deposited their "all you can eat" breakfast on the floor. Attacks rippled down one wall of passengers and up the next. It was a sickening relay race; I turned and fled.

The ship continued to roll until we were out of the stormy channel. The skies brightened outside Freeport which raised our spirits and morale. Bill was a shade of swamp green when he came up on deck.

We stood at the rail to watch as docking began. The process dragged on for an hour as the ship maneuvered in and out of the pier area. Presently a group of native workers with hatchets and saws began cutting down a tree at dockside. One of the ship's officers finally admitted our ship was a substitute for the regular liner, temporarily in dry dock for repairs.

"This is a much smaller ship than the regular Sea Escape," he explained. "The configuration is not in synch with the docking area. The tree blocked our access; it had to come down."

Freeport was a disappointment. Large warehouses filled with souvenirs, including every conceivable way to carve a coconut, were lined up one after another. Overpriced strings of beads, baskets, straw mats, hats and bags were displayed unendingly. Bahamian natives in colorful dress manned the warehouse stalls. They added the only touch of class to the starkly commercial buildings; especially with their distinctive British accents.

We all met for ice cream and sodas after shopping and then it was time to catch the jitney that would take us back to the ship. Buoyed by the sunny weather on the island, we discussed going to the pool when we re-boarded.

"I think I'll have a Daiquiri before dinner," Kay said. "Want to join me?"

"Sounds good. Those native bartenders should make excellent drinks."

Departure from Freeport was late afternoon. We stood at the rail and listened to the steel drum band serenade us with its unique sounds and rhythms.

As we left Freeport Harbor and entered the Gulf Stream, without warning the skies got dark and the sea was immediately rough. Bill retreated to the stateroom; Kay and I abandoned all thoughts of a swim in favor of a drink in the lounge. Amey and Josh sat with us.

The storm quickly intensified and the seas roared and crashed against the small ship. It was hard to distinguish anything outside the windows except the tremendous swells that appeared and disappeared as the ship rolled from side-to-side and tossed from end-to-end.

Gravity worked overtime with each violent pitch of the ship and moved the unanchored lounge furniture like pawns on a chess board. Unchecked, they slid back and forth across the room. As if on a crazed carnival ride, we rode to-and-fro in our chairs afraid to stand up. All at once a fellow passenger was thrown from her chair. Unable to stop herself, she body-surfed across the floor where she struggled to her hands and knees and crawled from the room on all fours. The native bartenders, who might have had great mixology talents, only looked at us helplessly in this emergency.

"This has never happened to us before," was their explanation.

Josh left to check on Bill. Amey, Kay and I, scared we'd also be thrown from our chairs, stood up and clung to the poles that supported the ceiling. These provided subway-like handholds for the few that remained in the room.

During one of the ship's more violent shudders, the entire stock of glasses was swept from the bar shelves in a frightening crash. As if by centrifugal force, all the water swirled out of the swimming pool. The chairs raced across the deck and flung themselves helter-skelter into the vacated space.

That was enough for me and I urged everyone to move to the dining room where I remembered the tables were anchored to the floor. Forming a human chain, with Kay leading and Amey bringing up the rear, we inched our way to the dining room. We were just in time to witness a stack of china dinner plates cascade uncontrollably down the buffet counters and onto the floor in thousands of pieces. As carelessly as the passengers had been looked after, so had the ship's china.

We were never told about life jackets or life boats and I couldn't remember seeing either one. I was terrified and kept whispering a prayer over and over, "God, please save my children; God, don't let my children die." I alternated between fear and anger that the crew wasn't available to help and comfort us. Kay rationalized it probably took every man to keep the ship afloat in such a storm.

Four hours later we sailed out of the storm and back into Miami. Incredibly the stars and moon were shining; I thought I'd never see them again. The lights from distant causeways and other ships in port shone a bright welcome that seemed surreal after the experience we'd just survived. Had I imagined the storms in which we'd spent our day? Would anyone believe the tale of our escape from the sea?

As we disembarked, the officers stood shoulder-to-shoulder in spotless white uniforms. They waved goodbye to their departing passengers who were reduced to a disheveled mass - yearning to go free.

Too bad, Poseidon, a close call but this time Jonah came out a winner.

First Class Stowaways

Several years after the near-fatal voyage of the Sea Escape, Josh invited us to visit his speculation/fixer-upper house in Miami's Buena Vista section. He had literally turned rundown shabbiness into a real estate dream. Memories of the sit-up-all-night experience we'd endured on our previous trip forced the decision to book first-class tickets on a sleeping car.

As we boarded the sleeper in Pennsylvania Station, we were greeted by an elderly white-haired black man in full Amtrak uniform, even to gold braid on his cap. He asked for our tickets, consulted his clipboard and said, "Yes, ma'ams, Mrs. Fuller and Miss Amsden, Compartment 11. Right this way. I'm George, your sleeping car steward. I'll do everything in my power to make your trip pleasant and comfortable." I thought, this is too good to believe, and readily surrendered to the steward and his old-world kindness, courtesy and service.

Our compartment was comprised of bright stainless steel cupboards, shelves and cubby holes; two upholstered seats faced one another next to a large picture window. I was relieved neither Kay nor I was any bigger than we were. As it was, one of us would have to stand out in the corridor while the other changed for bed, washed and used the toilet. It was a good thing we knew each other well to exist in such close quarters for a day and a half. The biggest plus was the beds where we could stretch out for the night and a dining car for our meals.

George showed us how to access some of the important features of our space. He uncovered the toilet by raising the tiny sink and latching it to the wall. He demonstrated how to convert the two seats into a bunk. Then, with the turn of a handle overhead, he dropped the upper bunk which hung suspended from two sturdy chains. George's agility amazed us as he put one foot on the arm of a seat and sprang up to the bunk and down again, demonstrating the safest mount and dismount procedures. I knew I could never be that agile; furthermore I'd *never* get down out of the bunk in the middle of the night. I offered the upper to Kay who rose to the challenge with her usual affability.

She said teasingly, "But George, you might have to come back at bedtime tonight and give me a boost. Is that part of your job?"

The old man chuckled. "Yes, Ma'am. Y'all need anything, y'all just ring that buzzer right there." He pointed at a small red button clearly marked, "Call Steward".

We closed the compartment and settled into our seats to watch the station platform slide by as we crept along the underground tracks out into bright sunlight. The train quickly got up to speed and we raced southward.

I decided to get comfortable until dinner and, slipping off my shoes, relaxed knowing we didn't have to think about anything except crossword puzzles and gin rummy games until we reached Miami.

All of a sudden I sensed we were not alone in the compartment. Had I been dozing and was confused by our new surroundings? It could happen; age was a factor in all things. But no, there *was* a faint scuffling near my feet. I looked down just in time to see two mice race for cover. Undoubtedly, the stowaways had been living in the cubicle long before we checked in.

Although I am proud of my innate fearlessness where mice are concerned, I urged Kay to press the "Call Steward" button. George announced his presence with a discreet knock.

She opened the door and said, "George, I thought this was a *private* compartment."

"Yes, ma'am."

"Well, it isn't. There are two mice in here with us."

I was sure George's ebony face showed traces of reddening, but he was composed as he said, "Ma'am, I'd move you to another compartment but the train is full. You want me to set a trap? We got plenty of those. Or, I could see if there's any coach seats available."

I thought, how could this be possible? We had paid handsomely for our accommodations only to discover we would be sharing them with two rodents. Obviously George knew the mice were regular travelers. The threat of going back to coach status was too ominous to deal with and I told him, "No traps. No coach. We'll share the space."

## To Miami with Love

The house Josh so proudly welcomed us to was testimony to his incredible sense of design and creativity. The two-bedroom ranch was filled with cool colors and comfortable furnishings. Fresh flowers were in every room. A board fence enclosed the backyard which not only provided a safe haven for his little dog, but afforded privacy when eating on the deck. The yard was filled with beautiful new plantings, but Josh was most proud of the centuries old banyan trees which, he said, were what "sold him the place".

Kay and I were laden with housewarming gifts we had carried from New Hampshire in our tote bags. The loaf of maple oatmeal bread baked the day before we left home made the biggest hit along with the container of maple butter.

I always thought Miami was a vacationers' mecca. But when Josh took us on the computerized monorail that runs from one end of the city to the other, I was surprised to learn the Brickell section of Miami is home to international banking institutions and multinational corporations.

We rode the monorail to Vizcaya, the winter retreat of industrialist James Deering. He had imported the building materials for the mansion from Italy for what was to become an Italian renaissance marvel. Now, all thirty-four rooms were turned into a museum. Originally an open-air home overlooking the Atlantic, it had been enclosed with glass to protect the furnishings yet still preserve the view. We especially enjoyed the many-tiered garden that extended behind the house as far as the eye could see.

We shopped for souvenirs at Bayside Marketplace, Miami's answer to Boston's Quincy Market. We had a cold drink in the atrium and watched elegant pleasure boats tie up at moorings on the waterfront side of the market. I thought, what an experience it must be to go shopping in a luxury craft at such a beautiful venue.

Traffic in Miami was heavy, frantic and dangerous. Even with "walk" signals on the traffic lights, pedestrians were targetted by impatient motorists who issued a challenge at every intersection - especially to these two confused older ladies obviously from out of town. We felt

70

like "marked" women as we window-shopped along Collins Avenue.

At a particularly high-traffic corner, somone nudged my arm. I looked down to see a petite elderly woman clutching a purse and two grocery bags.

"Cross me," she commanded.

"Excuse me?" I asked.

"Get me across the street. I could get run over if I try to get to the other side by myself." She pulled me out into the street like a human shield, then pushed and tugged my arm until she had steered us to the opposite corner. Without as much as a nod of thanks, she disappeared into the maze of shoppers.

"There we go in another ten years," Kay commented.

## Miami Beach

Across the Julia Tuttle Causeway from Miami, sandwiched between Biscayne Bay and the Atlantic, is the Art Deco world of South Beach where tourists triple the size of the residential population. Lining one side of Ocean Drive, a spectacular array of restored hotels, dating to the 1920's, offer an unobstructed view of beaches, palm trees and ocean. In an ultimate fashion show, deep colors of bougainvilleas and hibiscus contrast with the pastel geometric motifs of the buildings. In the pre-World War II era, the *Arts Décoratifs* style swept the country and became the hallmark of design in cities up and down the East Coast.

We walked the length of Ocean Drive to Government Cut where multi-decked cruise ships entered the Atlantic from the Port of Miami. So unlike Sea Escape, these "carnival" vessels, adorned with brilliant streamers and twinkling lights, were as tall as highrise buildings and magnificent to see.

## Ego Trip

The new Lincoln Road Mall had become a serious contender with Ocean Drive for tourist dollars. Cars are banned for blocks allowing the public to walk freely among pricey boutiques and relax in open-air cafes.

Josh performs his magic in hair and makeup design at Ego Trip on Lincoln Road. Considered a prime location, the classy salon is a major attraction for young movers and shakers of Miami and Miami Beach. It was here I spent the last day of our vacation having my hair cut and styled by my son.

During his beginning studies at beautician school, Josh had used me as a guinea pig for practice facials, haircuts, sets and perms. Now he was a consummate professional who had taken advanced courses in Paris, New York and San Francisco. He was sought-after as a designer for fashion magazines, catalogs and television commercial photo shoots. I felt like Cinderella.

## All Aboard

The train trip home was pleasant and comfortable. At a stop-over in Washington, D.C. passengers were invited to step out on the platform to stretch their legs.

After fifteen minutes the conductor called out, "All aboard!"

We turned to do his bidding just as eight last-minute passengers dashed across the platform to our train.

"RATS!" we all shouted and, in a brief moment of panic, we rushed en masse toward the entrance of the sleeping car. Then, with a collective sigh of relief, we saw the repulsive group jump down below the underbelly of the sleeping car.

"What if they get into our compartments from underneath," I said.

"Don't worry," Kay offered. "They're only apt to come around after dark; we get off before that." I searched for some obscure comfort in what she said.

## The Perks of Aging

After retirement there are many perquisites in watching one's years accumulate. We particularly appreciate the luxury of being free to decide at the last minute to take a day trip to one of our favorite places in New England, especially if having a beautiful day is key to its enjoyment. Geographically, we live in a part of New Hampshire that allows easy access to some of the best sights and sounds around.

We love to watch the sun rise at Ogunquit Beach in Maine. If the spirit moves us and fine weather is the promise of the day, we make the decision to go. Called "beautiful place by the sea" by the Abenaki Indians, Ogunquit is a haven of golden beaches and exquisite scenery only forty-five minutes from home. In warm weather we walk the beach for our morning mile, in and out of the shallows left by the receding tide.

Because it has so much to offer, Ogunquit is a favorite year around day trip. The Marginal Way footpath follows the shoreline, and no matter how many times we take this walk we find something to exclaim about as each twist in the path reveals a new and spectacular vista. Here we can watch the ocean alternate from stunning bursts of spray as it crashes against the rocky cliffs, to serene blue-green reflection of cloud patterns.

Perkins' Cove, the prize at the end of the Marginal Way, was once an artists' colony. Today the inlet, with its vista of sea, rocks, fishing boats and stately homes is a picturesque cluster of gift shops, galleries and restaurants. It is the timeless quality of the natural beauty surrounding this point of land that draws us back time and again.

We can be at L. L. Bean's Freeport, Maine, shopping headquarters in an hour and a half. Our lifestyle ranges somewhere between rustic country, relaxed cosmopolitan and go-to-church. Bean's always has what we're looking for to dress up our old duds. In addition to clothing and outdoor gear, there's a cafe in the store. We always spend time over coffee and a muffin, bagel, scone or biscotti, all delicious. Comfortable tables and chairs allow customers to relax, review shopping lists and exclaim over purchases already made.

Bean's is open twenty-four hours a day, 365 days a year and, because we're early risers, we ordinarily get there by 7 a.m. On the way home, if we haven't indulged too much at the cafe, we treat ourselves to lunch at the original Weathervane Seafood Restaurant in Kittery. It's always a difficult decision between lobster stew and fried clams - with bellies, of course.

The other end of the spectrum, the White Mountains of New Hampshire, is also only an hour and a half from home. Another year-round day trip.

When we were in our fifties, cross country skiing was a favorite winter sport and the groomed trails at the foot of Mt. Washington in Bretton Woods, were our first choice. The mountain, with its crown of glistening snow, is the essence of all wintertime scenery. Since my fractured ankle made me afraid of falling, instead of skiing we now hike the trails that skirt the Mt. Washington Hotel. These wind around the property in the sunlit glow of New Hampshire's famous landmark.

We make an annual trip to Polly's Pancake Parlor in Sugar Hill, New Hampshire. Timed just before the fall foliage season floods the state with tourists, Polly's waffles are the reason we make the trip. Whether served simply with butter and maple syrup or all dolled up with ice cream and elaborate toppings, this is what waffles are all about. Ordinarily we take Route 93 north through Franconia Notch where

Dressing up our old duds

New Hampshire's state symbol, the Old Man of the Mountain, keeps his eye on the goings-on. Not far up the road is the aerial tramway that climbs Cannon Mountain, carrying skiers and sightseers alike. I rode it once as a child but now my fear of flying includes tramways and ski gondolas as well as planes, so I enjoy the Notch from the safety of the highway.

Boston, Massachusetts, is only a two-hour bus ride which, in our opinion, is the only way to go. Once there, we use the "T", the city's public transportation, to move around. We enjoy the theater, Red Sox baseball and Quincy Market.

Kay treated me to "Phantom of the Opera" for my 70th birthday. Because we had ridden the bus to the city, I just assumed we'd get home the same way. To my surprise and delight, she had a limousine waiting when we stepped out of the theater. As the audience streamed out into the cold, windy January evening, I knew we were the target of envious glances. I tucked my arm in Kay's and we made our way past a line of cars to our waiting chariot.

"What a treat. I was dreading the bus ride."

When we were settled in the luxurious warmth of the limo, Kay said, "I thought our aging bodies deserved it."

I leaned my head back against the seat and thought how very right she was and how special she had made me feel.

Primarily because of its openness and acceptance of all lifestyles, Provincetown, Massachusetts, has drawn us back for years. Because it's a five-hour drive, we stay at least two nights, usually in the Coastal Acres campground near the end of Bradford Street.

Provincetown's Race Point sits at the tip of Cape Cod. Here we watch the sun rise out of the sea in the east and, in the evening, see it disappear back into the water on the western side.

We park our RV for the day close to the pebbled beach at Herring Cove where I brought my mother so long ago. This is a place to unpack our folding table and beach chairs, enjoy the scenery and eat a light lunch. Wonderful footpaths weave their way for miles through sand dunes which provide plenty of good walks. In the evening we mingle with the crowds that roam the length of Commercial Street and succumb to the blatant tourist traps. A dish of Ben & Jerry's ice cream is particularly delicious when eaten on the benches outside the town hall known affectionately as the "Meat Rack".

In our preretirement days, there were occasions when Kay made solo trips to a weekend professional conference or I went to a function that kept me away overnight. Each of us was disturbed by these separations although it wasn't until retirement moved us away from those demands that we actually talked about it.

Kay said, "I didn't know what to do with myself when you weren't here. I felt like half a person."

When left alone we kept notes of small events that passed through our day, things we wanted to share with each other when we were reunited. No one else would find them interesting, but by then we knew how each looked at life.

The number of times the dog got into the cat's litter pan. A sports article in the paper carefully clipped and saved. A new detour in the road that added fifteen minutes to a simple five-minute trip. What Josh had to say when he called, or Amey when she stopped by. We looked forward to reading those pages of notes even though some had lost their zip in the excitement of the homecoming.

I would look at Kay when she returned from a trip. I tried to read her face and see in her eyes the story of her feelings as she came through the door. I saw nothing but love.

Getting home is always the best part, whether forced to travel alone or on trips together. There is a quality of peace that home provides, a quiet place to talk about thoughts and feelings, a comfortable haven where words are unnecessary, a sanctuary where nobody hears the drums or sees the dance.

# TRAVELS WITH DOLLY

*"...at seventy, an overactive bladder means at least something in your body is working..."*

Anonymous

## A Borderline Breakdown

"Lady! You can't come through here. This is for motor vehicles only." The armed and uniformed border guard waved his hands over his head and ran from his kiosk like the last defender at the Charge of the Light Brigade. I wondered what he was so frantic about; he was only protecting the customs station where Canada meets the U.S. What threat did an elderly woman pose, unless of course he thought I was carrying a weapon or contraband some place on my body he couldn't see. I ignored him, and with my head high and determined steps, continued to advance on the kiosk.

It was raining and I was drenched. I'd walked a half mile from where Kay sat in our new 32-foot Dolphin recreational vehicle that unexpectedly and stubbornly refused to go another inch.

I told myself, "You should have known better. You brought bad luck the last camping trip. Why'd you think anything had changed?" Soaking wet, I plodded along the highway toward the border feeling much like the Biblical character that jinxed every expedition he went on.

Faced with this new crisis, it took very little effort to recall that other hapless camping adventure twenty-five years before. It was my first camping experience and I had taken on a trip so ambitious it issued an open invitation for bad luck to accompany us. The number of misfortunes that befell us were outdistanced only by the miles we traveled without ever reaching our destination.

I had planned to drive to California and back in three weeks. Along the way numerous obstacles arose, and I was forced to abort the trip at the Grand Canyon.

Bad luck began the very first night as we camped on the shore of Lake Erie. Rain leaked in the rear window of our rented Dodge Jamboree RV soaking my bed. Misfortune road with us into Tom Sawyer country where Amey had an asthma attack in Injun Joe's Cave. It camped with us in Oklahoma where we watched in horror as a mini-tornado gathered up the four corners of our picnic tablecloth and spun it away with the food we were just about to eat. It took on the face and jaws of a southwestern fire ant which hid in my moccasin and chomped down on my toes. Pain skyrocketed up my driving leg and forced the loss of a day's allotted mileage.

Total breakdown of the Jamboree took place on an Indian reservation in Thoreau, New Mexico. It was late in the afternoon; the Indians were well into their firewater. They edged closer and closer to "white squaw with two papoose". I was about to take defensive action and get my one wagon in a circle when we were saved by the cavalry that arrived in the form of a tow truck from Albuquerque one hundred miles to the east. It was the only vacation I'd ever been on where I lost weight.

The current crisis in which Kay and I found ourselves differed from my first in many ways. We had traveled to Nova Scotia to research my forebears, the Wentzel family, who migrated from Holland in the late 1700's. They settled on the Le Havre River in Pleasantville near the fishing port of Lunenburg. Kay had done careful preplanning which resulted in an enjoyable trip.

Most of our research was done in Halifax, the capital of Nova Scotia. This jewel of a city is perched on Halifax Harbor with the Atlantic Ocean broadening out beyond. The vital statistics of all Nova Scotia residents - past and present - are lodged in the city hall. A cross-hatched maze of gardens, interspersed with benches and shade trees, bloomed in an exquisite burst of color near the government buildings.

Kay helped me work through endless reels of microfiche on which were stored the marriages, births and deaths of my maternal ancestors. Most families have a secret somewhere in their annals. My great-grandmother turned out to be mine as records from 1863 disclosed she was three months pregnant on her wedding day.

Nova Scotia was not just a step back in time for me. My memories of the excursion also include the panorama of tiny inlets and expanse of seacoast that came into view around every turn in the road, my daily "fix" of herring in sour cream and breakfasts of eggs and finnan haddie. A special takeaway memory was crossing the Le Havre

River on a small ferry perhaps at the exact spot where my grandmother had ice skated across as a child.

This was the Dolphin's "maiden" outing and not without growing pains. During a torrential rain, we had serious leaks around the windshield and the back window over and into the bed. The sewage level in the holding tank misregistered on the monitor panel and waste backed up around my feet and ankles during what became known as the "shower from Hell". But it was on the homeward leg that the engine's solenoid wire fused itself in the wrong position. It was that last greedy stop, at just one more gift shop, that had rendered us "dead in the water".

The U.S. Customs kiosks at the New Brunswick check point appeared closer than they actually were. It had looked like only a short walk from where we sat in our luxurious ark of the highway, which we called "Dolly". Never one to skimp on quality or quantity in any purchase, Kay had acquired an RV large enough to accommodate a crowd. It floated along the highway riding beautifully and smoothly. It wasn't going anywhere now, although Kay tried over and over to get the starter to catch. In my proactive voice I said, "It's 4 p.m.; we're not sitting *here* all night. I'll walk up to the border crossing to get help." I had already covered half the distance when the rains came.

"Lady, get out of the road. Look behind you," came the excited guard's renewed orders. When I looked back I was amazed to see a line of cars slowly following in my soggy wake.

"I'm very sorry," I said, "but I need to get help. My RV is broken down back there. I need to call a tow truck."

"Just get out of the way, lady. Amazing you weren't killed walking in the road like that. Use the pay phone in the office but I can tell you this..." Somehow I knew here came another message from a man anxious to put a female in her place; especially an old wet one. I was right. He continued, "...U.S. garage people don't do work in Canada, and I know for a fact a Canadian tow truck won't pull you through to the states."

I called a dozen garages before I found one in Houlton, Maine that agreed to come. We were pulled through customs and into the U.S. on a slow tow with all wheels remaining on the ground because Dolly was so much heavier than the tow truck. Once we were across the border, the driver and his helper crawled under Dolly and succeeded in jump-starting the vehicle. They advised us to drive straight through to New Hampshire without stopping.

"Lady, you can't walk through here"

"Don't shut off the motor," was their parting advice. We had no intention of stopping and sped off into the night down I-95.

Our joy at being restored to drivability only lasted a short time as the headlights began to dim; then abruptly were gone entirely. Only very weak hazard lights worked and we were reduced to a frustrating crawl in the breakdown lane. When we saw signs for a truck stop we pulled in. As instructed, we left the motor running while we asked about repair facilities.

"No one here now. Will be at 7 a.m. Someone'll help you then; get you right back on the road for sure. Stay right here overnight. It's okay to shut off your motor, we'll have you back on the road in no time."

Parking in a truck stop overnight, in the company of rumbling eighteen-wheelers with the aroma of their exhaust, made sleeping impossible. The semi's were on timers that automatically started and stopped their motors at exasperating intervals. In the morning, we were tired, groggy, but hopeful when the repair crew came to inspect Dolly.

Three attempts to repair the solenoid and six hours later, we'd had it. Dolly was towed to a dealership for further diagnosis. We rented a car, drove home and returned for Dolly two days later.

Although she was up and running, Dolly's solenoid was not the only problem. There was no guarantee she was one hundred percent, or ever would be. On the way home we made a detour to a Four Winds recreational vehicle dealer. We had decided owning another Dolphin was too much of a gamble.

The infamous Ma Barker had nothing on Kay and me that afternoon. As we pulled into the display lot I said, "Don't turn off the motor whatever you do."

"Don't worry. I'll just let them think I'm old and forgot it was running. Get out, let's browse."

We made a snap decision on a 24-foot Class C Four Winds. The salesman was generous when he saw the pristine condition of the barely used Dolphin we offered in trade. If he'd known we didn't dare turn off the motor and that the deal included two full holding tanks of sewage, his delight might have been tempered. The "Ma Barker gang" kept those facts to themselves and drove off in their new recreational vehicle.

A Gold Medal Event

The first voyage of the Four Winds took place the following

year as we headed south to Charleston, South Carolina. Although it was late March, snow was predicted; we left a day early hoping to out-run the storm. Two and a half hours from home we found ourselves mired in snow and spent the night in a motel.

The first time we actually camped was our second night out in Jonestown, Pennsylvania. The Four Winds was eight feet shorter than the Dolphin, a factor that greatly increased maneuverability in driving and parking. The "house" portion of the RV took the length reduction much less gracefully.

We had forfeited the Dolphin's king-size bed in an airy room for a closeted, wall-to-wall double bed in the Four Winds, now referred to as Dolly II. In fact, it was so cramped we had to crawl into bed up over the foot. We tried to ignore this difference but at our ages, once our bladders were bedded down in a horizontal position, they shifted into overdrive. Like ships in the night, one of us was always crawling out to the bathroom as the other crawled back in.

Getting into bed was minor compared to the challenge that waited in the bathroom where the difference in vehicle length was most apparent. Once inside the lavatory, the space between the closed door and the toilet was barely ten inches; the same length as my feet. This made alighting on the commode an event of Olympic proportions. Overweight to begin with, I instantly filled all the available space in the room and in fact, was trapped nose-to-door. I managed to inch down the lower half of my clothing then, hoping the toilet lid was up, I dropped my body into a sitting position, banging my dimpled knees into the door on the way down. The reverse process was worthy of the gold medal as, with quivering leg muscles, I struggled to lever myself upright. I rose at the speed of unleavened bread making desperate grabs for my underpants and slacks on the way. If I accomplished this in the dark, I awarded myself *two* gold medals.

## The "'Monbacker"

Kay planned the itinerary for all our trips. She was the undis-puted captain of our ship, did most of the driving and all of the park-ing. She was also in charge of hooking up to campsite water and elec-trical outlets. She carried out all these tasks with great efficiency. It was a *thing* with her to be self-sufficient and independent. She was espe-cially sensitive to interference from male campers who surreptitiously watched her from the vantage of nearby campsites. When she didn't cry for help, their egos had to have been crushed.

One evening, as she tried to hook up the water hose, an errant faucet repeatedly sprayed her in the face. A woman unexpectedly appeared from an adjacent campsite and whispered to her, "My dear, I really don't think your husband would like you to be doing that. Why not let him take care of it?" Later, when we had finished laughing over the incident, we wondered what had motivated her. Was it that Kay had white hair? That she was female? Or that the woman had a husband who kept *her* wrapped in cotton?

Campgrounds have two types of sites: back-ins and pull-throughs. It takes great finesse to back a large RV into a campsite but Kay was equal to it. She couldn't do it alone however, which allowed me to exert my skill as a 'monbacker.

The 'monbacker stands at the rear of the RV, facing the vehicle, clearly visible to the driver in one of the rearview mirrors. It was also important to have a comprehensive view of trees, rocks, other RV's, dogs, children *and* the dreaded male in the next campsite. I raised my beckoning arm with the elbow slightly bent, fingers upright. My legs were two feet apart which conveyed the message of complete nonchalance to all observers.

My first shout of "'monback" was packed with power as it set off the RV's backward motion. My arm movements were carefully coordinated with loud cries of "'monback, 'monback"! I constantly shifted my head and eyes as the vehicle approached, to be sure no low-hanging trees wiped out the TV antenna or roof vents. Once the RV was secure in its space, the 'monbacker's job was over. It was a satisfying contribution and I savored it to the fullest, all the way to my glass of wine at happy hour.

Charleston

The James River Campground sits across a causeway from Charleston proper. Ringed by remnants of centuries old live oak trees and limbless torsos of once stately pine, the trees were stark reminders that a devastating hurricane had passed through two years before.

Daily roundtrip jitney service was available to take us from the campground to the wonders of Old Charleston. We took advantage of the service every day. We thoroughly enjoyed a conducted tour the first morning. After that, we jumped on and off a sightseeing trolley if we wanted another closer look at one of the city's landmarks.

The number of churches was impressive. Each an architectural wonder in itself, spires, domes and turrets reached for the heavens above the city. We marveled at the staircases, shaped like hearts, that reached out from the front doors of antebellum mansions. Iron bolts and other modern structural devices had been added to the houses as protection from hurricanes. Fort Sumter sits in the harbor opposite the city's signature pastel houses. It is a timeless panorama.

A life-size replica of the *H. L. Hunley,* displayed outside Charleston's historical museum, was the hallmark of the trip for us. The first of its kind, this diminutive submarine sank the Union warship, *Housatonic,* during the Civil War. The volunteer nine-member crew powered the propeller with handcranks; the captain manned the dive plates. The *Hunley* rammed the side of the warship with a metal spar and a 135-pound torpedo. The concussion of destruction that followed sank the Union vessel and the *Hunley* as well. All hands on both ships were lost. (At this writing, the *H. L. Hunley* has been recovered from the depths of Charleston Harbor. The entombed crew are to be given a full military funeral.)

## So Long, Dolly

On our return from Charleston, Kay wasted no time getting to the RV dealer where she traded Dolly II and her knee-bruising bathroom for a 29-foot Four Winds. The new vehicle not only had a larger bathroom and vanity, but a bedroom with a queen-sized bed approachable from both sides.

We spent a weekend at the Laurel Lake Campground in Fitzwilliam to test it out. Dolly III was comfortable and spacious without being cumbersome. In short, she was an excellent compromise between the luxury of the original Dolphin and the cramped interior of Dolly II.

We wintered the RV in a storage area near our home in Rochester, New Hampshire. To protect the vehicle from New England's long season of ice and snow, Kay purchased a blue tarp. The package was so large and heavy, it took two of us to carry it to the car and then unload it on the ground next to Dolly. Once the wrapping was removed, we began unfolding; we unfolded and unfolded some more until we had enough blue tarp to cover the infield section of Fenway Park. Either Kay's math skills had failed her or the package was incorrectly labeled.

We walked around it several times strategizing the best way to hoist it up on the top of the RV. Kay climbed onto Dolly's roof dragging a portion of the tarp with her; I walked alongside with another portion held over my head to ease the drag. We repeated this operation several times and managed to fold the tarp back on itself, but yards of it still trailed on the ground. Dolly was completely hidden.

We crawled along on opposite sides of the vehicle's underbelly. Our heads brushed the pavement as we peered across at each other and tossed the grommet ropes back and forth under the chassis. We tied our respective ends to anything that offered itself and ended with a sloppy job that resembled a large blue bubble.

As usual we had put the task to be done ahead of the potential physical strain on our bodies. I was bent double and forced to cling to Kay's arms for support. Like "pushmi-pullyu" we slowly made our way home.

Our Rules of the Road

At our ages we need routine and follow a travel regimen that works for us -

```
300 miles a day is enough
6 a.m. on the road
8 a.m. off the road for breakfast and to get out of the way
        of commuters
10 a.m. rest stop
Noon  lunch and avoid lunchtime commuters
2 p.m. rest stop
4 p.m. check into campground; set up camp
        HAPPY HOUR - watch other campers move in;
        cook and eat supper
Take a long evening walk around the campground to jog heart
        rates made sluggish during long day of sitting; meet other
        campers and pick up camping ideas, places to stay and
        what to see and do
```

Decompressed in Ocala

The destination for our next trip was Punta Gorda, Florida, near Port Charlotte. Two days before our departure over a foot of snow had fallen, burying Dolly where she sat packed for the trip. We used ladders, stepstools and roof rakes to clear the snow and got away on schedule.

Just north of Starke, Florida, Kay reached to turn on the air conditioner and triggered a shriek from under the hood. It was the unmistakable rasp of metal against metal.

"Oh God," I said. "Either I really am a Jonah or we are ghastly victims of voodoo and black magic. All I have to do is think about camping and the wheels of doom start turning."

"We're almost to the Starke KOA; perhaps they can suggest a place to get it looked at."

The campground owner was paternalistic in his helpfulness. He eyed us up and down, but never showed a hint of scorn or uttered a sarcastic word about two elderly ladies traveling alone in such a large RV. Instead, he looked under the hood then picked up the telephone and made arrangements for us to bring Dolly in right away. My gratitude overflowed; I could barely keep from bowing my way out of his office. We were relieved for several reasons. Uppermost was any delay could jeopardize our reservation at the RV resort in Punta Gorda.

As it turned out, the problem could be diagnosed but *not* repaired at that garage. It would require at least a half a day at the Ford dealership ten miles south. Luckily we'd be headed in the right direction.

"The compressor's gone," was the official word.

"Can we drive without it?" I wanted to know.

"Nope. Engine'll burn out if you try that. Plus you can't use your AC and you'll need it down here."

We spent the day sitting and standing around a garage in the middle of nowhere while the repairs were made. We had our dog on a leash and even if there had been shops to browse in we wouldn't have been welcome. Eventually we completed our trip to Punta Gorda.

Our campsite was on the transient side of the park, more expensive to rent but on a scenic inlet that came in from the Gulf of Mexico. The full essence of Florida at its most picturesque - boats bobbing on the water, gulls screaming overhead.

It was our first time at an RV resort and we took advantage of all it offered and enjoyed the pool, jacuzzi, barbecues and campfires. The number of "snowbirds" who made the resort their wintering place and the individuality of their campground housing was an education.

We walked the perimeter of the entire park morning and evening, past travel trailers of all shapes and sizes as well as traditional motor homes. The majority would never set tire to road again; rather they had become quasi-homes of the highest order; some boasted picket fences, outdoor patios and, the most positive indicator of permanence, trees, shrubs, perennial plants and here and there, a fountain. "Park models", a new style of stationary campground housing had the look of a cottage with all the compact qualities of a motor home.

The "startrekkers" came out at night. Traveling alone or in pairs, these were residents who rode up and down the resort roads on bicycles, adult tricycles and in golf carts. Handcrafted models of steam engines, airplanes and school buses also came by. These could carry up to six people who all laughed and waved to the onlookers. The products of many hours in the resort hobby shop, these clever conveyances were mounted on go-carts and we looked forward to seeing them come by.

We left our "calling card" each time we departed a campground after a stay of a week or more. This is a polite term for dumping the RV's sewage holding tanks. Black water came from the toilet; gray water from the bathroom and kitchen sinks. The rule is dump the black water first, then the gray which flushes out the sewer hose.

The dumping station often had a waiting line and we had learned the hard way the importance of efficiency. Dumping is an unpleasant, but vital task which involves hooking one end of the RV sewer hose to the outlet under the vehicle and placing the other end in the dump station in-ground receptacle. Kay would hunker down and connect the hose underneath Dolly while I kept my hand on the outgo end. On this particular trip, we had not yet used the hose. Coiled up in winter storage it had become brittle and developed a series of pinhole cracks.

Tiny fountains of sewage sprang out of every hole in the hose when Kay pulled the plunger to release the black water. I wanted to run away and hide. This urge was quickly replaced with a desire to slap the faces of the men watching and smirking from the RV's waiting behind us.

"Don't you dare let go of your end." I knew Kay spoke through clenched teeth.

Unhurriedly and with considerable savoir-faire we finished our chore and drove off in a cloud of composure we didn't feel.


Two for Mangrove Mama's

KOAs, or Kampgrounds of America, are dependable places to camp. Independently owned and managed, they are inspected annually by teams of quality control professionals out of their Billings, Montana headquarters. The discovery of a KOA resort in Sugarloaf Key, Florida was exciting and we determined to make it our destination the next time we traveled.

Our trip south was without incident that year. The drive out to the Keys was a breathtaking experience, especially the views from the Seven Mile Bridge that connects the upper and lower Keys.

The "Startrekkers"

The resort was situated on an inlet from the Atlantic. It also was a haven for "snowbirds" with many of the same signs of permanence we'd seen in Punta Gorda. Sugarloaf is at milepost #20 making it twenty miles north of Key West. We had reserved a waterfront site where sandy beaches were spread with comfortable lounges, individual barbecues and thatched gazebos.

Across the inlet, flocks of pelican roosted in the mangrove trees. The ungainly birds, with their enormous pouch-like beaks, swayed in the dense branches and eyeballed the water for their next meal. Airborne, they took on a style and grace that belied their bulk. They swooped low and dive-bombed into the water rising with pouches sagging with fish.

We took the bus into Key West and rode the sightseeing Conch Train. We took snapshots at the Southernmost Point of the United States and reflected on the Cuban refugees who had floated in at that point of land. We feasted on stone crab and experienced the famous sunset celebrations at Mallory Square.

Outside the campground, a short walk across Route 1 took us to an exceptional restaurant, Mangrove Mama's. The exterior was typically Spanish with red tile roof and stucco walls. A series of small dining rooms inside led onto a spacious patio open to the sky. Giant palms and mangrove provided shade and shadow; a small adjacent building housed an intimate cocktail lounge and bar.

Wooden tables and chairs, painted glossy oranges, aquas and reds, were spashed with daubs of bright contrasting colors. Homemade tablecloths and napkins - none matching - were somehow in concert with the whole scheme. Abstract drawings, sketches and caricatures done by local artists were hung in planned disarray around the walls. The price tags were too steep for our pocketbooks and we contented ourselves with souvenir T-shirts that said we were each a "Mangrove Mama".

Drinks were delicious and generous. The menu offering of Caesar salad with grilled shrimp surpassed any I'd ever had. Much to the amusement of my dining partner and the waitresses, I ordered it each time we went.

Dawn was barely putting in an appearance the morning we packed up to leave. As I turned back to the campsite from my one last walk on the beach, the sun was still below the horizon, but its rise was foretold by incredible patterns of color that crept across the dark sky. Second-by-second the colors changed from deep golden orange to splashes of pale yellows all haloed by the approaching ball of fire.

As we tooled homeward through the endless length of Florida, I thought several times how trouble-free this trip had been. As if Dolly read my mind just then Kay said, "Uh-oh." I knew without a doubt my thought had escaped and once again the finger of fate pointed at us.

We were going around Jacksonville on the I-95 bypass when the speedometer needle began to flap erratically from 0 to 100. The vehicle behaved O.K. otherwise. It was only a short distance to our designated campground for that night so we kept going. The Yellow Pages offered the location of a nearby garage where we lined up with other customers early the following morning.

Diagnosis: A short circuit in the Automatic Braking System.

Treatment: Completely disconnect the ABS to stop the speedometer needle from flapping.

Prognosis: Full recovery once we got home to our own garage and could leave Dolly for a day or two.

Short Term Prognosis: To get home, we'd have to drive one thousand miles without a speedometer to register our speed and mileage. Assured that we could drive safely without the ABS, we got back on the road.

At first it was a game to gauge our speed. We jokingly tried to recall how fast the trees had gone by when we were doing sixty miles per hour. Then we noticed the Schneider eighteen-wheelers had a message just for us on the rear of their orange trailers. An "800" phone number was provided to report any excess of the fifty-five mile per hour limit. We put our trust in their drivers' integrity and tucked in behind them as often as we could. If we couldn't find a Schneider, UPS drivers were good at maintaining a steady pace. Kay added another checking system and began timing the distance between highway mileposts.

Her skill at driving in the face of adversity was our surest protection along with her ability to stay calm and deal with things. I, on the other hand, needed an exorcist.


John Berendt's Garden

RVers love to exchange information - about their vehicles, places they've been, best campgrounds, what to see and do.

In Charleston a few years earlier, fellow campers compared the attributes of that gem of South Carolina with those of Savannah,

Georgia. The comment we heard most was, "Only restoration better than Charleston, is Savannah."

It had not been possible to "do" both cities on that first trip; now was the time. What clinched our decision was the book, *Midnight in the Garden of Good and Evil* by John Berendt. We had both read it twice and thoroughly enjoyed the fiction-based-on-fact story about Savannah.

KOA had no campground near the city. "We'll stay at a Good Sam out on Tybee Island," Kay said as she referred to our campground guide books.

Anticipation was at its peak as we drove along the outskirts of the city and caught glimpses of things to come. We were headed for River's End Campground on Tybee, the recreational playground for Savannahians. Tybee Island is fourteen miles east where the Savannah River meets the Atlantic. The best thing going for it was the Crab Shack, "where the elite eat in their bare feet". It *was* a rundown shack but offered the best boiled shrimp we'd ever tasted.

As far as we were concerned, River's End Campground was the end of the world. There were no jitneys or buses to take us into Savannah. "We'll unhook Dolly everyday and drive in," Kay decided.

"What about renting a car?" I asked. "I'll check at the office."

Enterprise Rent-A-Car, a combo of taxi service and car rental, is a camper's saviour and solved our transportation problem. They collected us from Tybee and drove us to their headquarters where we did the paperwork and picked up a car. At the end of our stay, we simply reversed the process.

A marvel in restoration, Savannah broadcast a welcome from the glorious gardens that ring the city squares, to the gold dome of the old state capital building. Forefathers, appalled by the Civil War destruction of Atlanta, handed over their city when the forces of General William Tecumseh Sherman arrived on their doorstep. Although Savannah was to be occupied by the Union Army for the remainder of the war, Sherman honored his promise not to destroy it.

As we had done in Charleston, we took the official, narrated tour of the city on the first day. Then, with map in hand, we walked the streets revisiting areas that had piqued our interest and drew us back for a second look.

A milestone in city planning, Savannah's pattern of squares and parks was laid out in 1793 by its founder, General James Oglethorpe. In Forsythe Square, we sat on the bench made famous in the 1994 movie, *Forrest Gump*.

We returned several times to the Cotton Exchange. Once the headquarters for the purchase and export of cotton, it now housed unique shoppes and boutiques. Colorful banners and emblems fluttered in the breeze touting the shopkeepers' wares and vying for the eye of the tourist.

At one time wagonloads of raw cotton were hauled into the yard of the Exchange for presentation to the buyer factotum. This wizard, called the "factor", determined the purchase price as he eyeballed the cotton from Factor's Walk, an iron bridge that extended out over the wagons. The Port of Savannah, once the hub of cotton exporting, saw the bottom drop out of the business during a yellow fever epidemic. The abandoned waterfront warehouses have been converted to restaurants, food marts and specialty shops. Among these was the *Peanut Shop*, an oasis for nut addicts like myself. I came out laden with bags which I defensively justified by saying, "They're gifts."

The city had an ethereal effect on us. We could only imagine what John Berendt had experienced.

The Ices of March

As we made our way home from an almost perfect trip, weather forecasts of "fronts closing in bringing sleet and freezing rain", made inroads on our vacation-mode psyches. When we reached the Jonestown, Pennsylvania, KOA the accuracy of the forecast surrounded us.

"I'm too old to make this transition," I whined. Kay, exhausted and testy from the long day's drive, replied, "Twenty-four hours ago you said it was too hot. We've been someplace we've never been before; it was great. Now we're back to reality; stop complaining."

The next morning Dolly was encased in ice and it was still sleeting. Kay chipped away the thick coating, but it quickly regathered. I was antsy to get going but knew it should be her decision; she had to do all the driving. We finally started off after the busiest commuter hours.

We crawled to the interstate on secondary roads as Kay maneuvered Dolly's mega-tons on slippery surfaces and in poor visibility. It was frightening. One wrong move on her part and we could slide off the road. When we reached I-287 in New York, the sleet had turned to snow. We were surrounded by trucks that, oblivious to the weather, sped by throwing up thick slush on our windshield. Erratic drivers that show up at the first sign of a snowflake, were all over the road. I wanted to scream each time we struggled up a greasy incline or encountered merging traffic..

I finally gave in to my frazzled nerves and said, "Get off at the next exit. We're going to a motel for the rest of the day." I got no argument. We had been in our room fifteen minutes when I noticed a strange pattern on the inside of the window drapes.

"What's that light outside the window?" I asked.

Grasping the pullcord, Kay opened them. "My God," she cried in disbelief, "it's a new day: sunshine and blue sky!"

### So Long, Dolly - Again

We decided to rent a campsite for a year at Laurel Lake Campground in Fitzwilliam. A combination of sunny open fields and shaded pine groves, campsites were nestled everywhere. Included in the seasonal rental was winter storage for Dolly.

It was strange to return to the lake where I had owned property at one time. The campground was on the east side, whereas I had lived on the west. Otherwise I would have been overcome by nostalgia. The summer was crowded with activities involving friends and historical society events.

In October, Kay decided to dispense with Dolly's enormous blue tarp we'd struggled with for several winters. In its place she ordered a canvas cover designed for our particular RV model. It went on like a dream and, although we still had to crawl on hands and knees to secure the underbelly straps, we were happy with the result.

After a year off the road the travel bug bit us again. As winter's cold dismal days descended, that bite finally got our attention. We had some serious questions to resolve. Among them were the feelings of vulnerability we'd experienced as vehicle problems occurred a long way from home.

I had long been concerned about Kay driving a vehicle the size of Dolly III as well as all the outside hook-up work she did. Winter storage was a constant worry. Because of her size, Dolly had to be kept some distance from our house where out of sight, she had twice fallen prey to vandals.

*Family Coach Magazine* had an article about the RoadTrek, a classy travel vehicle barely longer than our Dodge Grand Caravan. In December a call to our favorite RV dealer confirmed that he had the latest models on his lot.

Kay and I each felt we had met our new best friend when we were introduced to the RoadTrek. Extremely compact, it featured all the amenities of Dolly III except inside "moving around" space. Driving and parking would be easier and the RoadTrek could also be used as a second car.

The convenience and luxury of something so small was astonishing: two bunks, *comfortable* toilet, microwave, refrigerator, two-burner stove and a sink, plus storage compartments, TV hook-up and air conditioning. All in something *only* twenty feet long. The hook-up process was streamlined and visits to dumping stations were eased by all the built-in features. Of course, she would still need the old fashioned 'monbacker.

"There's a price break if I purchase it now," Kay told me.

"Now? What about getting Dolly out of the campground in Fitzwilliam? There's a chain across the entrance and we'll need to clean her out before you can make a trade." As an afterthought I said, "There's snow and ice on the ground."

"Dolly's accessible to the main road because we're in site number one. I'll call and tell them we need to move her out; they'll take down the chain for us."

We again found ourselves faced with an almost impossible task. Winter storms had worked to our disadvantage and Dolly was surrounded by a field of ice. We crawled on the frozen surface to unbuckle the belly straps. I thought of what we asked our bodies to do and, at their ages, how well they responded.

"Pull the cover towards you," Kay directed from her side of the RV.

My feet were almost unmanageable on the ice but, by hanging onto Dolly with one hand, I reached up and grabbed a handful of the cover. I pulled but nothing happened.

"What are you doing over there?"

"I'm trying, but the cover won't budge."

Kay came around to my side and we pulled together. Nothing. "It's caught on something. I'll climb up and take a look," she said.

Terrified she'd slip and fall, I pictured the distance to our cell phone where it was locked in the van out on the road. What if I needed to call 911?

Halfway up the built-in ladder on the back of Dolly, Kay was eye level with the problem. A three-inch coating of ice had frozen the cover to the vehicle roof.

"Solid ice. Hand me the hammer."

"I hope you're not going to walk on the ice up there."

"I'm going to see if I can break this up. We've got to move Dolly out of here today."

I handed her the hammer but the ice was too thick to make even a dent. Here we had this sparkling day to move Dolly, but she sat immovable with the cover iced to her roof and hanging down around her windows.

"I think we should cut the cover off around that ice."

"With what? All I've got is my small Swiss Army knife."

"I've got a pair of scissors. Why not try?"

Kneeling on the roof, Kay began to saw around the canvas with the knife while I made intersecting cuts up from the bottom. The job was made difficult by our inadequate tools plus the ice on which we were forced to balance. Gloves got in the way and we had to work bare-handed. We were forced to stop frequently to blow on our fingers to get them warm.

Except for the canvas still thoroughly "iced" to the entire surface of Dolly's roof, with jagged fringes hanging all around, the bulk of it finally lay at our feet. Poor Dolly, she had served us well and it was sad to think of driving her in public in such a state of degradation.

We began our journey across the state. Once out in the sun, the ice started to melt and the loosened canvas flowed out from the roof like a flag of surrender.

Trading Dolly III for the RoadTrek was an inspired move, but it took us several camping trips and even more shouting matches to work out which one's turn it was to stay out of the way while the other made up the bunks or cooked meals. We found new meaning in the term "cheek to cheek".

Camping Hints for the Senior Sojourner

Compliment the driver - **keep her happy**

Give the 'monbacker all the credit for a good parking job - **other than cooking, it's her most important contribution**

Know the difference between the black and gray water holding tanks - **avoids last minute embarrassment at the dumping station**

Be sure the RV is level - **lest the bathroom door swing the wrong way in the dead of night**

Take your eyeglasses when you go to the shower - **to clearly read the length of time the water will run for the twenty-five cents you put in the meter**

Remember the color of your toothbrush - **particularly if you're traveling with someone over 70**

## Acolytes of Adventure

Kay and I are not unique in our desire and ability to make camping a pleasurable mode of travel. The joys and rigors of camping *are* appealing to older people. Some true gypsies live in their RV's year around and go from place-to-place as the spirit moves. These are often folks who have sold their houses and invested the proceeds in huge motor homes, some costing as much as a million dollars.

My personal camping history dates back thirty years to the pop-up trailer I purchased after I acquired the lake property. The kids and I lived in it in the woods while the cabin was being built. Thanks to Kay and our new RoadTrek, I had come full circle: back to a camping vehicle whose compact qualities dictated the need for a lot of outdoor living. *That* is camping.

### Reflections

There was a point in my life when I internalized everything. In fact, I spent twenty-five married years biting my tongue because that's how I thought a wife should behave.

Kay spent twenty years with an overbearing, manipulative woman she was afraid would walk away from her if she verbalized what she really felt. In the end, she lost her anyway.

An extension of our friendship has been the fertile environment we made for each other: nurturing support, trust and understanding that provided freedom to feel, think and express ourselves. Our bitching and growling at one another resulted in the discovery of other personae living inside our bodies who have struggled for years to be heard. That is what women can do for women.

Volatility needs to exist in a good relationship to keep it healthy. The beauty of a woman is in the passion she shows.

# DRIVEN BY TWO UNIQUE YANKEES

*"...think about what you can do each day to promote yourself
mentally, physically and emotionally..."*
Erma Bombeck

## A Horse in the Ladies' Room

A book on the bestseller list, any bestseller list, is the ultimate
for an author, especially a neophyte writer like myself. Who would ex-
pect a book about an eighteenth century New England inn to receive
such recognition? A book that told about the water that dripped through
the ceiling of a packed dining room from an overflowing second floor
shower? A book about the father of the bride who died in the inn
men's room while the wedding reception whooped it up in the adjacent banquet room? And what about the customer who filled her pock-
etbook from the evening buffet? A bestseller? It was either an incredible joke or a delightful dream.

No joke. No dream. It was my book, *A Horse in the Ladies'
Room,* which appeared in the number one spot on the bestseller list two
consecutive weeks at the largest book store in Keene, New Hampshire.
A most perfect reception for a book I had started to write shortly
after my sixtieth birthday and finished six years later.

I had quit my day job at UNH to fulfill the desire to write about
the years Red and I owned and operated the 1796 inn in Fitzwilliam,
New Hampshire. I wanted the book to be a tribute to my husband and
the legions of other hospitality professionals who manage to keep smiles
on their faces despite chaos reigning behind the scenes.

My desire to write had become a growing  presence since a
poem I wrote in second grade appeared in the school newspaper.
Even at the age of seven, I felt the thrill that comes from seeing one's
work in print. It was then the itch to connect words together and build
a book actually began.

For the fifteen years following Red's death, career and children made important demands on my time, but when Josh was out on his own and Amey a college senior, I saw my chance.

But you can't write about Fitzwilliam here in Rochester, I told myself. When I verbalized those thoughts to Kay she generously helped me pack my typewriter and, along with Red's diaries from the inn, I moved to the unfinished cabin. As memories of those hectic and humorous days spilled out of my mind, I began to write. It was a creative haven; a forest retreat surrounded by the dregs of a late spring snow and the coziness of the woodstove that crackled and hissed its encouragement.

## The Unique Yankee

Money was tight. I was living on a widow's Social Security benefit. By the following year I knew I had to find a source of income to feed both me and my writing addiction.

When I sold the inn fifteen years earlier I'd opened a small antique shop in Fitzwilliam Village which, because of its location across from the inn, did extremely well. I had named the shop the *Unique Yankee*. I decided to re-invent that business in the shed behind the cabin.

Kay was instantly interested, supportive as always. Although she was still teaching, her summers were free to help with buying and manning the shop. We dealt in small items, nothing as big as furniture and only what we cherished and would like to own ourselves.

It was fun to poke through yard sales. We would be lured off the road by tired household items that ran the gamut from old shutters, lamps and washing machines to shoe boxes of Legos forgotten and outgrown by a child. We were always on the lookout for old glass milk bottles, folk art and birdhouses.

At a weekly auction we joined local dealers inspecting the "good" stuff, speculating on "what'll it go for" and then bidding low on box-lots of junk. We almost always found a hidden treasure in these boxes, something that had once resided in glory on a mantlepiece, dresser or kitchen shelf, long-since replaced by a new-wave gimmick made of synthetic material. Human nature was to get rid of the old, bring in a slick new replacement and then start collecting the old again.

At flea markets, we timed our arrival to catch sellers as they unpacked their wares. We would split up and hurry from dealer to dealer, peering into the backs of trucks and station wagons or even sneaking a look through unpacked cartons. We were shameless and hid behind our white hair and wrinkles pretending complete innocence, believing they gave us license to pry.

Kay had acquired every antique guide available and carried these tomes with her in an old canvas tote that said "Have Bag Will Travel". She was as thorough in her research of values and pricing as she was in everything. My strong point was dickering but I relied on her advice as I went through the maneuvers of buying.

I'd start with, "What're you asking for *this*...?" I had learned to put emphasis on "this" in such a way "piece of junk" was inferred. If the response wasn't in our price range, I'd come back at the dealer a second time with, "I'll give you $...for it." This, I hoped, conveyed the message that I was being very generous with my offer. Usually the answer was, "I can't let it go for less than $..."; I'd counter with another offer until we came to terms. If the dealer refused to budge, and I really wanted to make the purchase, I'd give in. Otherwise I'd walk away shaking my head to let him know he'd lost the day's best offer. If we settled on a price, I'd ask questions to get some background facts to embellish into a bigger story when it was time for us to turn the piece around.

Kay had a passion and talent for finding old trunks, baskets, wooden boxes and crates as well as milking stools and other farm implements all covered with dirt and muck. She bathed them in Murphy's soap, sanded with fine steel wool then rubbed in a coating of mink oil. The gentle glow and patina she brought out in the pieces allowed us to sell them at triple what we'd paid.

Our boxes, especially those with colorful advertising labels, were so popular that a dealer from California, whom we met at a flea market, followed us back to the shed and purchased all the boxes we had in stock. She was a traveling "picker", purchasing pieces with particular customers in mind. "I have buyers on the West Coast that crave anything from New England. I'll have these sold as soon as I get home."

On one of our buying trips, Kay discovered a Victorian commode, or potty chair as they were often called. At first glance it appeared to be a low table, but a lid opened to reveal a square seat with a hole in the center. This also raised to allow the placement and retrieval of a chamber pot. Made entirely of oak, the top was beautifully beveled. We displayed the commode with the lid raised and brightly colored flowers springing out of the potty. It sold almost immediately.

The *Unique Yankee* should have been a business bonanza but our customer base was too small, primarily summer residents. There

"You want $5.00 for *that?*"

was not enough boost to my finances to supplement my income.

"We need to take our stuff where we have a bigger audience," Kay said. We began setting up at an outdoor antique show almost every Sunday.

You Know Who You Are

The first time we went to Howland's Antique Show in Amherst, New Hampshire, I called ahead to reserve a space and was told the dealers' gate opened at 7 a.m. Kay and I, disciplined Yankees that we are, took Howland's at their word and arrived promptly at 7. When we turned off the highway onto a side road circumventing the show field, we passed at least fifty cars already parked on both sides. Shortly the road divided; we could either go around to the left or continue straight ahead where a sign displayed the confusing message, YOU KNOW WHO YOU ARE. We looked at one another.

"Do we?" Kay asked.

"We know who we are because we reserved a space," I reasoned. "Go straight."

As we headed past the sign, a furor of voices arose from a group of people standing by their vehicles, "You're not 'You Know Who You Are'! Turn around. Go the other way, *to the end of the line.*"

Chagrined, we turned around and took the road that bore to the left. At least one hundred cars, vans and pickups were ahead of us. Each resembled a movable scrap heap with its load of furniture, lamps, newel posts, coal shovels and hay rakes precariously balanced and carelessly lashed on with worn pieces of clothesline.

All our things were carefully packed in the van. The sight of this total disregard for planning was an affront to my need for organization. I blurted out contemptuously, "They look like the Beverly Hillbillies. What is this place anyway?"

The line of vehicles started to move forward just as we reached the end. We made a quick u-turn and pulled in last. When we finally drove through the entrance gate and received our space assignment, I leaned across Kay and asked the attendant, "Who are 'You Know Who You Are'?"

"Dealers who paid in advance for the entire season. They get to drive on the field and set up first. If you only come once in a while, you need to get here by 5:30 a.m. to get a good place in the other line."

We learned our lesson well. We rose at 3:30 a.m., hurried to get ready and be on the road by 4. Often we drove off in such a rush Kay's hair was a blizzard of white tufts. Whenever I commented on it she would say, "I slept on it wrong and I don't care. *I* don't have to look at it and I'll wear my sunhat."

We discovered arriving at Howland's by 5:30 a.m. had another bonus besides getting through the gate early. The longer we sat in line, the more exposure our wares had to other dealers who came by the vehicles, looking into dark loads with flashlights and lighted matches. Some of the most important deals were made at that time; often hundreds of dollars changed hands. We quickly caught on to this process and packed our things so the best items were on top and easily seen. Kay stood outside to answer questions such as, "Anything in golf?" or "Any old tools?" If there was interest in what we had, she signaled me and I stepped out to do the "dealing". A comraderie developed among the early arrivals that we looked forward to, an empathy for what we'd all gone through to collect the things we were selling, each item carefully chosen to attract both dealers and retail buyers.

We loved setting up our displays. The table cover with its bright red, blue and green checks provided just the right "country" backdrop for our antiques. Wooden boxes stacked off to the side with tools on them so carefully arranged they looked as if they were tossed there. Lesser items were spread out on a tarp on the ground. I always took a bunch of artificial flowers to attract customers to our booth.

We packed our lunch to avoid the temptation of over-spending calories at the snack bar. Fruit was the main staple: blueberries Kay picked from the wild bushes around the cabin were mixed with cantelope, kiwi and grapes. Tossed with a dressing of honey and yogurt, then topped with her homemade granola it was an everlasting nutritious favorite. We sat towards the back of our space near the van's tailgate and watched the people as we ate, exchanging whispered comments about the potential buying interest of each.

With ESP running full tilt, we *willed* buyers to turn in at our space. We would peer out from under lowered eyelids without moving our heads and observe "lookers" as they browsed. We knew just how long to wait before we said anything; even as innocuous as "Good morning." If we moved in too fast or said too much, we could drive people away who liked to look without fear of hard-sell tactics. We dreaded women who picked up, fondled and cooed over something, then put it down saying, "I'll have to ask my husband."

This annoyed me and I'd moan to Kay, "Oh, God; another one. You wait and see: if they come back, he'll say to her, 'What do you

Peering up from under lowered eyelids

want that thing for?' and kill the sale. Some women still live in the dark ages."

Selling was a different game than buying. We were aware we'd never get rich, but were determined to make something on every sale. Although we knew how much we'd paid for a piece and could estimate market values from our reference books, we usually priced by the seat-of-our-pants. In the long run, this method worked amazingly well.

We tried to hook customers by spinning elegant stories about the origin of our things. People stood open-mouthed as we described the barns and attics we had combed to unearth the very piece they held in their hand. We could barely contain ourselves when we closed a deal. Kay would grin at me and say, "We should be ashamed to tell stories like that."

Howland's stayed open through the October foliage season. Despite complaints from our aging bones, we forced ourselves out of warm beds into the cold reality of Sundays at 4 a.m. We had to wear mittens as we chatted with other dealers in line. Our breath came in froths of steam that quickly swirled away in the brilliance of the sunrise.

We were overcome by the ambiance of fall in the show field. The fiery trees and deep azure sky formed a backdrop for dealer displays and the chatter of stolling crowds. The aroma of hotdogs and French fries filled the air. Selling antiques took a back seat to the euphoria of being a small part of the spectacular carnival.

Strawberry Acres

I couldn't safely stay in the cabin beyond November 15th; the terrain was too treacherous as the ground froze and snow came. Then a group antique shop opened in Fitzwilliam. The shop owner would handle all transactions and record them on each dealer's balance sheet. At the end of the month space rent was deducted from sales. The dealer was paid the excess or coughed up the difference in rent still due.

I decided to rent a small booth and moved my inventory from the shed to Strawberry Acres Antiques. Rather than close the Unique Yankee and do without any winter business, I could now be an absentee dealer, check on my sales by telephone and restock as needed.

It wasn't long before there was a second reason for doing business year-round. When I left UNH I was not yet eligible to collect my own Social Security and sign up for Medicare so my health coverage was transferred to an insurance group known as COBRA.

"I've got to get rid of these exorbitant premiums," I told Kay. "Every extra penny I make goes for health insurance."

The state insurance commissioner's office suggested New Hampshire Blue Cross and Blue Shield. Among other plans, the brochure described group coverage for small businesses with less than ten employees. The Unique Yankee qualified and for the next few years I enjoyed health benefits at a reasonable rate. We continued our buying trips and traveled regularly from Rochester to Fitzwilliam to restock the booth.

Financially, my outgo was still greater than my income. I was forced to return to UNH as a temporary employee. My experience with the university's computerized accounting system was valuable and transcended all departments. I was moved from place-to-place on campus to fill in during maternity leaves and other short-term absences.

All of my assignments were enjoyable as well as lucrative. Most memorable was ROTC Administration, an adjunct department of the university for student reserve officer training. "I'm in the Army now," ran through my head as dozens of UNH students in battle dress uniforms paraded by my desk.

The colonel in charge, to whom I reported, was a stickler: there was the army way and then *there was the army way*. Each time he approached my desk, I felt the urge to jump from my chair and snap off a salute. Where was the informality of academe I had come to cherish? Fortunately the woman I was subbing for had her baby sooner than planned. At a farewell breakfast I was presented with a hooded sweatshirt with A-R-M-Y emblazoned across the front. The jacket remains a reminder of my greatest battle.

Keeping "KALM" on New Passages

My work on *A Horse in the Ladies' Room* had slowed considerably, but never stopped entirely. The book was completed six years later and I was proud of what I'd accomplished.

Now what? I knew my manuscript needed editing. Where was I to find that kind of professional help? How would I get the book published? Should I have an agent? If so, where would I find one?

I spent long hours in the library wading through literary journals, publishing guides and writers' market places. I came away confused and discouraged.

"This is just a book about an old New Hampshire inn," I wailed

105

to Kay. "Why do I need all those headaches. I simply want to tell the story; to have a legacy for Amey and Josh; to leave a little of myself behind."

How childish and petulant I sounded, how self-centered and egotistical. What, I asked myself, do you want to have happen with this book? The answer was, I want people to know what Red and I did, what a challenging and rewarding job innkeeping was. Red used to tell people how we worked twenty-four hours a day, *eight* days a week. I wanted to show why those years were some of the happiest of my life.

Hesitantly I asked Kay to look over my manuscript. Was this being fair to her? She was *my* dearest friend and I was asking her to critique the writing of *her* dearest friend. How would that work? Could she be honest or would she only give it lip service in the interest of preserving our relationship? Could I gracefully accept her editing without throwing a protective tantrum when she deleted a description I felt was perfect? Would I feel obliged to accept her editing because she was the professor to whom I had submitted a term paper hoping for a decent grade?

I received my answer when she returned the first chapter covered with purple marks. I was angry at first but soon came to welcome and appreciate the consideration she'd put into each notation and recommended change.

"Let's talk about these," she said. Every suggested deletion, rewrite and alteration was examined and discussed. I either agreed with her assessment or stood my ground in defense of my words. As a result my phrases became tighter, the humor more distinct and the stories all the more exceptional.

When the rewriting was complete, Kay said, "I think we should publish this book ourselves."

Shocked I said, "And then? How are we going to sell them?"

"We'll take it one step at a time," she replied.

Each with a notebook, we visited local bookstores to gather information on details we needed to know to build *our* book. We looked at different sizes, bindings, covers, paper and number of pages. We compared book prices. We examined frontispieces such as copyrights, forewords and tables of contents. We explored the mysteries of ISBN, the International Standard Book Number that identifies each book and its publisher for the entire world.

We found back covers were valuable space for important sales teasers. We decided to use "How to be hospitable when the guests keep getting in the way" for our book about innkeeping.

Our heads were full of ideas, and the book became an extension of ourselves. We thought of little else except how it should look and feel as well as the readability factor. Once these decisions were made, we went to our local printer.

We had settled on 150 copies as the maximum we could possibly sell. "No one's going to pay money for this book; it's really just a vanity thing," I kept saying.

When the printer handed us his quote I felt sick: it came to $12 a copy and the rest of our overhead expenses weren't even included. "Why not do 300 copies," he suggested. "That will bring the per book cost down to $7 each." With much apprehension, we agreed.

On the way home I said, "We're never going to sell all those; they'll be packing them in the casket beside me."

When the books were printed and bound, I acted as my own agent and public relations person and began to call on local book buyers. With great temerity I would extend a copy of the book and ask if they would purchase a few, perhaps for their section of New Hampshire humor, history or even local authors. The response was amazing. I was flattered and experienced a tremendous sense of validation just to know seasoned buyers of books were going to purchase mine. I was even invited to have a book signing and reading which they would advertise.

At my first signing event I was nervous but encouraged and pleasantly surprised by the number of people assembled, each carrying a copy of my book. Was this really me sitting here, my adoring readers waiting in anticipation? I felt exalted beyond all expectation. As I settled myself, Kay stood off to the side to take pictures of this, the greatest moment in my life. I began to read.

Slowly I became aware of an unmistakable sound coming from the audience. Snoring? Not at my reading. *Please, don't let this be true!*

My eyes searched for the offender. Yes, there he was: head back, mouth open. Gone. The woman next to him caught my glance and hung her head in embarrassment. I instantly felt worse for her than for myself and her plight actually helped me to continue. Kay's photo of my attentive audience, with a gaping mouth in the middle row, did wonders to deflate any ego I might have developed.

Christmas brought such a boom in book sales, we ran out of our first run and had to place an a.s.a.p. request for another 300. Later in the year we had to order a third run. At this writing we are in a fourth printing of this book.

WMUR, New Hampshire's primary television station, asked to do background filming at the inn for their evening art and entertainment show. They would feature *A Horse in the Ladies' Room* and its author. Such excitement to see and hear myself on the air. My mother put it all in perspective by asking, "Who would have thought *you'd* be so prominent?"

Once the ink started to flow, a second and third memoir followed. *Where Lame Donkeys Lie*, is based on the discovery of family art, prose, diaries and love letters in an heirloom desk inherited from my grandfather. I wove the story together using the creativity of the owners as my inspiration.

*On the Wings of a Unicorn*, the story of my first marriage, was extremely painful to write as I revisited and disclosed secrets locked in my heart for decades. It was a healing process and through the book and the acceptance it received, I was able to reach out to other women with compassionate understanding.

## Two Unique Yankees

Before our first book was published we asked each other, "What are we going to call ourselves as publishers?" We tossed around several choices but settled on KALM, as much because it combined our initials as the reminder to keep "CALM" at all costs.

In our third year of business we had learned so much in our trial and error approach to getting books in print and marketed, that we wrote and produced, *How to Build a Book - Produce, Publish and Promote your Creative Work in Ten Successful Steps*. This pamphlet incorporated everything we had found out the *hard* way. We were inspired to write it to smooth the path for those just breaking into the world of self-publishing and marketing. Kay always says she likes the tenth step best: "Open the champagne the first time someone actually pays money for your book".

The realization that writing and self-publishing are considered crafts led us to get involved in pre-Christmas craft shows. In contrast to Howland's outdoor show where we had sold antiques, craft shows were enormous, elegant extravaganzas. Set in main-floor rooms and hallways of large hotels in major New Hampshire cities, space rent was high, but the exposure to four thousand plus Christmas shoppers all under one roof was priceless. The shows were loaded with sophistication; dealers were referred to as "vendors". Unlike dealers, we learned vendors don't dicker - they have a sales pitch.

Our display was carefully orchestrated with shelves, racks and large posters of each book cover. We encouraged passersby to pick up a bookmark and we offered free KALM Publishing pens.

Christmas music filled the air. Holiday lights twinkled throughout the display rooms and were repeated a thousand times over in mirrors and glass surfaces lucky enough to catch their reflection. Artificial snow was part of many vendor booths; especially those selling toys and decorations.

"I feel like a sugar plum fairy," I observed.

## WWW. KALMPUB.COM

Fifty years ago the word computer was new in everyone's vocabulary. "Univax is coming," was the cry heard around the bank where I worked in the 1950's. Employees were tested to determine which ones on the staff had a flair for math and logic. High scorers were labeled "Programmers". Immense climate-controlled spaces were set aside for Univax and when it arrived, only a certain few cryptographers, in hush-hush tones, were allowed to approach the alien. Today, everything anyone ever dreamed possible is accomplished on a desktop marvel known as a "PC".

Dot.Com was unknown to us when Kay and I formed KALM Publishing. We were still back in the dark ages using a word processor to produce manuscripts that weren't camera-ready.

We finally caught up with the times, picked up the telephone and ordered a Gateway PC. When the boxes with their Holstein cattle décor were stacked in our tiny living room, we asked ourselves, "Now what have we done?"

"We're not opening these boxes until we get someone here who knows what they're doing," Kay decreed.

"Oh, come on. Let's just take a peek." The temptation was too great and she quickly capitulated.

Unlike many mail orders, all the parts were included and went together smoothly. Kay read the directions while I made the cable connections, inserting the unmistakable red, blue and black males into their female counterparts. In two hours it was running, including the printer.

The PC is our only official piece of office furniture. We use our five-foot dining room table as a partners' desk. It's only when company comes that we get out laundry baskets and pack up the mess of papers and books to uncover the table beneath. As the door closes behind our departing guests, like two pigs anticipating the comfort of their mud-filled sty, we wallow with delight in reclaiming the table with its disarray.

Two years ago we had to put an extra leaf in the table so we could spread out more. If business expands, we still have another leaf in the storage shed. The only difficulty with that is our arms aren't long enough to pass things back and forth unless we get out of our chairs and walk around the table.

"We need a pneumatic tube like they used in old-time department stores," Kay said jokingly.

A vase of dried flowers always stays in the dead center of the table. A boundary marker of sorts.

After the Shouting

Humor inspired *Sisters by Heart - Partners in Aging*. After the crises and the near catastrophes, when the shouting died away, there was the ability to laugh - together, at ourselves, at one another.

Humor has eased the load, lightened the moment and turned the wrinkles upside down.

Without a doubt, the reservoir of adrenaline that has built up in us is the result of the fun and satisfaction we have derived in over twenty years of applying our individual talents to a common goal.

The name tags we wear when we're presenting a workshop or sitting behind our display at craft shows, read "Partners in KALM Publishing". What the tags don't say is that we're also partners in life.

In the heat of the moments that we are in the public eye, I can feel Kay's eyes. I can feel her smile. I can feel her pride.

If I'm making a sale, reading aloud from one of my books or behind the microphone at a podium, I don't dare respond to those vibrations. I could lose my place or my train of thought, but I know she's *the wind beneath my wings*.

Life has to have meaning. Being important to each other is just one of the ways we bring meaning to our lives. We have found serenity and great contentment in the challenges and pleasures we have shared.

With age has come wisdom and integrity and the ability to speak our minds. It's no longer a secret that we live for each other.

# PATCHWORK

*"...the days of our lives are 70 years...teach us to count our days*
*that we gain a wise heart..."*

Psalm 90


The very first esoteric experience we shared was a rainbow. For us that arc of colors symbolized God's pleasure with our budding partnership.

§

We were born in the 1920's and along with other women our age, have risen out of subservient positions and a patriarchal society. Women play a significant and independent role in the present and will continue to be defined in unimaginable ways as futures come to pass.

§

Kay calls herself a "singleton", not an old maid. "That's a stereotype," she says; "it only makes me think less of myself. I never wanted to be appended to a man; I'm a person, damn it. Marriage would have suffocated me. For you, getting married was like joining a club. You and I have a partnership that's far better than either of your marriages. We're joined at the heart."

§

Our church is important because it provides a sanctuary of opportunity to sit in quiet communion with our spirituality.

§

When I was a child my mother lied about her age. She wanted to be thought of as younger than she really was. I was a grown woman when she finally confessed. I have learned it's *how* you are old that matters.

§

We're fortunate we can still walk three miles a day.

§

I wondered if spilling soup down my front is an aging thing? Kay teased and said I should use a bib.

We were in a restaurant and watched a woman at the next table remove an oilcloth packet from her purse and place it next to her fork. When her meal was served she shook out the piece of oilcloth and placed it around her neck. Kay gave me a kick under the table, rolled her eyes toward the woman and mouthed the word, "BIB."

§

I was launched into menopause at the age of forty-four. The unhappy process hung around for ten years. Estrogen was a help with hot flashes: those sickening rushes of heat as if a pilot light ignited deep in the core of one's body.

With my metabolism in chaos, just looking at food packed on weight. The doctor intoned, "You can only eat twenty-five percent of what you ate before." It was a death sentence.

As if that wasn't cruel enough, along came osteoporosis and spinal compacting. My height dropped from 5'11" to 5'8". Recommended weight kept pace accordingly. The race between shrinking height and weight charts began and has yet to end.

Kay transitioned smoothly through menopause with nary a flash. No loss in height. No gain in weight. I watch her devour cake, cookies and ice cream while I nurse a pear and eat ten carefully counted chocolate animal crackers.

§

We respect the crones within. They are the keepers of our wisdom.

§

We don't let the numbers of our years dictate what we do, what we enjoy and what we think. We spread that philosophy whenever we can.

§

Our mental powers are amazingly elastic. The excitement of learning and doing something new is exhilarating.

§

Studies show affection is a basic human need that persists from infancy throughout life. Hugs see us through good times and bad.

§

*"...do not go gentle into that good night; old age should burn and rave at close of day..."*
Dylan Thomas

# RECKLESS ABANDON COOKERY

from
TWO WELL-SEASONED SISTERS

# INTRODUCTION

There is an important intimacy about food. In much the same way that Feng Shui plays a vital role in the arrangement and selection of home furnishings, sensuality is central to menus and meal preparation.

In earlier years, especially when the cabin was so much a part of our daily living, we took picnics to the waterfront, ate on the deck with our feet propped up on the railing or sat on pillows on the floor around the coffee table.

Kay and I, like most New Englanders, are food-oriented people, discussing what to have for dinner while we're still eating breakfast.

When we travel in Dolly, we make enormous lists of food to prepare at home and pack in two-meal-size Tupperware containers which can be easily "nuked".

Even today we are apt to make a ceremony of our meals, depending on the entreé. One is never too old for dinner by candlelight; on the other hand, supper on TV tables in the living room can be just as grand.

We have selected our most oft-repeated favorites to share.

# APÉRITIF   FORETASTE   ANTEPAST

Whichever descriptor one prefers, it all comes down to
whetting the appetite.

## SWEET 'N SOUR MEATBALLS

Use your favorite recipe to make cocktail meatballs.
Heat together one jar grape jelly and one bottle chili sauce.
Add meatballs. Serve in a chafing dish or other warming pot.

~~~~~~~~~~~~

## PIGS-IN-A-BLANKET

Wrap pieces of pickled watermelon rind in
half-slices of bacon - fasten with toothpicks.
Bake at $425^0$ until bacon is crisp.

~~~~~~~~~~~~

## CHEESE SAUSAGE BALLS

1 lb. bulk sausage   2 cups sharp cheese, grated
3 cups Bisquick

Blend together very well with hands.
Form into small balls. May be frozen.
Bake at $350^0$ for 25 minutes.

~~~~~~~~~~~~

# SALADS

Also known as hodegpodges or mixed bags, the stereotypical
salad has lots of greenery. These two are distinctly diverse types and tastes.

## MARINATED GREEK SALAD

*This keeps well and can be served as a separate garnish with an entrée,
or on lettuce as a side salad.*

Marinade: I cup white vinegar   I Tbsp. dill weed   2 Tbsp. sugar
I/2 tsp. salt   I/4 tsp. pepper   I/4 cup water   I/2 cup vegetable oil
Salad: 2 boxes cherry tomatoes   I lb. large mushrooms
I pkg. feta cheese, crumbled

Mix marinade ingredients. Place veggies and cheese in a plastic
storage bag and add marinade. Refrigerate I2 hours or longer and
turn bag often.

~~~~~~~~~~~~~~~~~~~~~~

## WALDORF SALAD

*We like to serve this as a separate course rather than as a
side salad with a meal.  Serves 8-I0.*

8 red Cortland apples (cored, but not peeled; cut into bite-size pieces)
I cup seedless green grapes, halved
8-oz. can pineapple chunks, drained (reserve juice)
I/2 cup diced celery   I/4 cup  walnut bits
Dressing: 8 oz. lowfat  lemon yogurt
I/2 cup lite mayonnaise   2 Tbsp. pineapple juice

Mix dressing ingredients in medium bowl. Add  to fruit mixture stirring
until well coated. Chill a few hours before serving.

~~~~~~~~~~~~~~~~~~~~~~

# BREADS

Bread is the main support of a meal, especially if it's a
tea party and served with Marmalade Butter.

## MARMALADE BUTTER

4 Tbsp. butter blend, soft    2 tsp. orange marmalade    I tsp. honey
Blend all together until creamy.

~~~~~~~~~~~~~~

## OATMEAL-RAISIN SCONES

2 cups flour    3 Tbsp. brown sugar    I tsp. baking powder
1/2 tsp. baking soda    1/2 tsp. salt    1/2 cup butter, chilled
I 1/2 cups oats    1/2 cup raisins    I cup buttermilk

Preheat oven at 375°. Combine flour, brown sugar, baking powder, baking
soda, salt. Cut in butter til mix resembles coarse crumbs. Stir in oats &
raisins. Add buttermilk; mix with fork til dough gathers in a ball. Turn out
to a lightly floured surface - knead 6-8 times. Pat dough into a 1/2-inch
thickness. Cut into 8-10 wedges & place on <u>ungreased</u> cookie sheet.
Sprinkle with cinnamon & sugar. Bake 20-25 minutes.

~~~~~~~~~~~~~~~

## MAPLE OATMEAL BREAD

*This bread traveled overnight in my tote bag to Miami by train. It's a "taste of New England" gift - enjoyed and appreciated by all recipients. A container of maple spread makes a delicious accompaniment and travels well.*

2 cups scalded milk    3 Tbsp. butter    I cup oats    2/3 cup maple syrup
I/2 cup warm water    2 eggs    2 tsp. salt    2 pkg. yeast    6 cups flour

Dissolve butter in warm milk & water - pour over oats - let stand 15 minutes.
Stir in syrup & eggs. Mix yeast & salt with half the flour. Add to first mix. Stir
and knead in rest of flour til smooth & elastic. Cover; let rise til double.
Punch down; form 3 loaves; let rise again. Bake at 325°
for 30 minutes or til done.

~~~~~~~~~~~~~~~~~~~~~~~

## GOLDEN BLUEBERRY CORNCAKE

*Be generous with the lemon extract - it brings out the blueberry flavor.*

3/4 cup cornmeal    3 tsp. baking powder    I cup flour    3/4 tsp. salt
I/3 cup sugar    I cup milk    2 Tbsp. oil    I egg, well beaten
I tsp. (+ a few drops) lemon extract    2 cups blueberries(add last)

Mix all dry ingredients; add milk, egg, oil, lemon extract - mix well.
Add blueberries. Put in greased 9x9-inch pan. Bake at 425° for 20 minutes.

~~~~~~~~~~~~~~~~~~~~~~~

# ENTRÉES

The main course, star of the show and culinary masterpiece,
comes on after an entremet of soup or salad.

## EASY AND RELIABLE ROAST CHICKEN

3 1/2 to 4-pound whole chicken (Perdue is definitely the best) - wash
inside and out, pat dry.   Sprinkle cavity with garlic salt.   Tie legs - set
wings.   Roast 1 3/4 hours at 375⁰.   Baste every 20 minutes with one
Tbsp butter or margarine melted in 3/4 cup Marsala cooking wine.

~~~~~~~~~~~~~~~~~~~~~~~

## GRILLED SWORDFISH

*This can be cooked under the broiler in a conventional oven, but
it's far better when done on the outdoor grill.*

1 lb. swordfish    Mayonnaise (lite or regular)    Lemon pepper

Liberally spread mayo on one side of fish; shake on lemon pepper. Put
fish on hot grill, mayo side down. Repeat mayo and lemon pepper on top
side of fish. Grill 7 minutes per side.

~~~~~~~~~~~~~~~~~~~~~~~

## VIDALIA ONION PIE

*This is a delicious way to serve an already elegant onion.*

1 cup saltine cracker crumbs    5 Tbsp. oleo, melted    2 Tbsp. oil
2 1/2 cups Vidalia onions, thinly sliced    2 eggs    3/4 cup milk
1/2 cup grated cheese    Salt & pepper to taste

Combine crumbs & melted oleo; press into a deep glass pie pan or quiche
pan - bake at 350⁰ for 8 minutes - set aside. Sauté onions in oil til tender
(do not brown) - place in pie shell. Mix eggs, milk, seasonings - pour over
onions. Top with grated cheese. Bake at 350⁰ for 45 minutes.

~~~~~~~~~~~~~~~~~~~~~~~

## BEEF BURGUNDY

*This is a great "company's coming" elegant stew that serves 6 people. We like it over rice or egg noodles and served with a big tossed salad.*

8 Tbsp. butter    2 cups sliced onion    I cup flour
I tsp. garlic powder    I tsp. onion powder    2 Tbsp. paprika
2 bay leaves    1/2 tsp. thyme    Salt & pepper to taste
4 lbs. stew beef, cut in 2-inch cubes
2 1/2 cups Burgundy wine    I can beef consommé

Sauté onions in half the butter; put in Dutch oven. In separate kettle, heat consommé and wine on low heat. Mix flour together with garlic and onion powders and paprika; dredge beef cubes in flour; brown in remaining butter (add more butter to pan as needed.) Put browned beef in Dutch oven. Pour consommé/wine mix over beef and onions; add bay leaves and thyme. Cook two hours in 350⁰ oven.

~~~~~~~~~~~~~~~~~~~~~~~

## ORIENTAL CHICKEN WINGS

*This recipe, served in candlelight, brings out not only the Chinese flavor of Feng Shui, but is the essence of the sensual aspects of a meal.*

I cup Lite Soy sauce    1/4 cup sesame oil    1/4 cup dark brown sugar
1/4 cup vegetable oil    2 lbs. chicken wings
2  one-gallon food storage bags

Cut off wing tips; discard. Wash wings and pat dry. In a glass bowl mix all sauce ingredients. Put wings in doubled bags; add sauce. Refrigerate all day: turn bag twice to distribute sauce thoroughly. Put wings plus 1/2 cup of sauce in a 13x9 pan. Cook one hour at 350⁰.

~~~~~~~~~~~~~~~~~~~~~~

# MARY LOU'S MEAT LOAF

*This is a delicious hot entrée; but we still like it best the second
day - cold in a sandwich!*
*Before starting to put this together, set the oven at 400⁰, wash your hands,
remove your rings and push up your sleeves!*

Put all of the following in a large bowl:
2 lbs. hamburg (1 lb. leanest; 1 lb. next leanest)
3 tsp. Gulden's mustard    1 raw egg    4 slices stale bread, pulled into bits
1 med. onion, chopped    1 tsp. salt    1 tsp. pepper    1/2 cup milk

Using your bare hands, squeeze and fondle the mixture until well
blended. Use non-stick spray on a 9x13 pan (glass or other.) Put mix
in the pan and mold it into a loaf. Bake one hour at 400⁰.

Heat a can of undiluted Cream of Mushroom soup, add a dash of
Worcestershire. Pour over meat loaf slices to dress up the presentation.

The next day make a sandwich for lunch - slice the meat loaf
thin; spread bread of your choice with relish, mayo and/or ketchup.

~~~~~~~~~~~~~~~~~~~~~~~

## FISH CHOWDER

*This is made in layers in one large kettle - better if made the day before. Kay's cole slaw makes a nice side dish.*

I onion, chopped    1/2 cup butter (I stick)   2  large potatoes, cubed
2 lbs. cod or chowder fish    I  sm. can evaporated milk
I  qt. whole milk    Salt & pepper to taste

Sauté onion in butter until light yellow, add potato - add water just to cover potatoes; simmer until al dente. Wash fish; add whole pieces to kettle on top of potatoes. Cover kettle. Cook until fish can be flaked apart (about 10 minutes.) Add entire can of evaporated milk; add whole milk as necessary (depends on how you like it.) Add salt & pepper. Simmer uncovered until milk is hot.
Serve with common crackers split in half and floated on bowls of chowder. These are an old-fashioned staple, but still available in most stores.

~~~~~~~~~~~~~~~~~~~~~~~

## LENTILS AND BROWN RICE

*Like beans and other legumes, lentils are a great meat substitute. This is a delicious winter meal which we like to serve with a jellied salad.*

3/4 cup lentils    1/2 cup brown rice (not instant)    1/2 cup chopped onion
I clove garlic, minced    I tsp. oregano    1/2 tsp. basil    1/2 tsp. thyme
1/4 tsp.marjoram    1/2 cup white wine    2 cups chicken broth or water
1/2 cup shredded Swiss cheese    8 thin slices Swiss cheese
Salt & pepper to taste

Mix all ingredients except cheese slices into casserole dish. Cover. Bake in 350° oven for I 1/2 hours or until liquid is absorbed. Stir after 3/4 hour. At end of cooking time, top with cheese slices, return to oven uncovered until cheese just begins to melt.

~~~~~~~~~~~~~~~~~~~~~~

## FRYING PAN STEAK FOR TWO

*This is steak at its sexiest - new twist on the way mother used to fry it. Great with a baked potato topped with guacamole.*

2 Delmonico steaks (about 3/4-inch thick)
I Tbsp. McCormick's steak seasoning
2 Tbsp. brandy, whiskey or apple juice
I Tbsp. Worcestershire sauce
I Tbsp. butter
I Tbsp. vegetable oil

Heat butter and oil in large (I2-inch) non-stick skillet on medium heat. Rub one half the seasoning well into one side of the steaks; put them in the skillet seasoning-side down; rub remainder of seasoning in top of steaks. Cook 5 minutes per side for medium. Remove to warmed plates. Add brandy and Worcestershire sauce to skillet; stir and simmer 30 seconds. Pour over the steaks and savor the eating!

~~~~~~~~~~~~~~~~~~~~~~~

# POTATOES

*We eat a lot of baked red-skinned potatoes with lowfat sour cream or plain yogurt. We also have brown or white rice often. Starch adds zip to a meal. Young's in Durham, New Hampshire, has the best restaurant homefries in the state.*

## HOMEFRIES

*We use leftover baked potatoes and leave the skins on for added flavor.*

6 medium potatoes, sliced crosswise
1/3 cup chopped onion    2 Tbsp. each: butter & virgin olive oil
1/8 tsp. paprika    Salt & pepper    Dash garlic powder

In a large non-stick frying pan over medium heat, melt butter with oil and paprika. Add onion and potatoes; sprinkle lightly with salt, pepper and garlic powder. Use a spatula to turn potatoes occasionally until crusty and brown and onion is soft - turn carefully to keep slices from breaking.

~~~~~~~~~~~~~~~~~~~~~~

## SLICED BAKED POTATOES

4 medium potatoes    I tsp. salt    2 Tbsp. melted butter
3 Tbsp. chopped fresh herbs (parsley, thyme, chive or sage) or 3 tsp. dried herbs (your choice)    4 Tbsp. cheddar cheese, grated
I 1/2 Tbsp. Parmesan cheese

Peel potatoes if skin is tough - otherwise scrub & rinse them. Cut potatoes in thin slices but not all the way through (use a spoon handle to stop knife.) Place potatoes in baking dish - fan them slightly. Sprinkle with salt; drizzle with butter; sprinkle with herbs. Bake at $425^0$ for 50 minutes. Remove from oven - sprinkle with cheeses. Bake another I5 minutes or til lightly browned, cheeses melted and potatoes soft inside.

~~~~~~~~~~~~~~~~~~~~~

# VEGETABLES

*During the World War II years, vegetables from my mother's Victory Garden were the main staple of our dinners. She also dug dandelions and pulled up weed-type grasses that grew in the field behind our house. Some were pretty unappetizing when cooking reduced their once vibrant greenery to a lifeless state. Still, we ate them all.*

## MOTHER'S PICKLED BEETS

2 lbs. small, cooked beets (reserve juice)
I small onion, halved and thinly sliced (half-moon shapes)
I cup sugar (can use less depending on individual taste preference)
I cup beet juice reserved from cooking
3/4 cup cider vinegar
I 1/2 tsp. salt    Dash pepper    2 bay leaves    12 whole cloves

Place drained beets in glass or china bowl. In saucepan, combine all other ingredients. Bring to a boil; reduce heat and simmer 5 minutes. Pour over beets. Cool and cover. Refrigerate 48 hours to thoroughly marinate.

~~~~~~~~~~~~~~~~~~~~~~

## GREEN BEANS CAESAR

*This is a delicious way to dress up a garden favorite. (I like anything with the word Caesar in it.)*

2 lbs. fresh green beans (cooked, I-inch pieces)    2 Tbsp. oil
I Tbsp. chopped onion    Garlic    I Tbsp. vinegar    1/4 tsp. salt
Fresh pepper    2 Tbsp. dry dark bread crumbs    2 Tbsp. Parmesan cheese
I Tbsp. butter, melted    Paprika

Toss beans with oil, vinegar, onion, salt, garlic, pepper. Put in ungreased casserole. Mix bread crumbs, cheese & butter. Spread over beans. Sprinkle with paprika. Bake uncovered at 325⁰ for 35-40 minutes.

~~~~~~~~~~~~~~~~~~~~~~

# ZUCCHINI-TOMATO GRATIN

*This is fun to make and a good way to use up all that zucchini!*

2 Tbsp. olive oil    I sm. red onion    3 med. zucchini
3 plum tomatoes    3 cloves garlic, minced    I/2 tsp. salt    I/4 tsp. pepper
I Tbsp. fresh thyme <u>or</u> I tsp. dried thyme    3 oz. Gruyere cheese, grated

Lightly oil 8-in. round baking dish. Slice onion into rounds; slice zucchini
and tomatoes to I/2-in. thick.
In large skillet warm 2 Tbsp. olive oil on med. heat. Sauté onion & garlic
til translucent (5-8 min.)
Place zucchini slices on edge around sides of dish (cut side against side
of dish). Place tomato slices against the zucchini. Place some of the onion/
garlic mix to hold the vegetables. Repeat the rows. Place remaining vegetables in center. Sprinkle with salt, pepper, thyme, cheese.
Bake 25 minutes at $350^0$.  Serves six.

~~~~~~~~~~~~~~~~~~~~~~


# FRENCH FRIED EGGPLANT

*We love Eggplant Parmesan, but this recipe will introduce you to the
wonderful taste of eggplant out on its own.*

I med. eggplant, peeled, cut into 3/4-inch slices
2 cups cooking oil    2 cups plain bread crumbs (in shallow bowl)
I egg, well beaten (in another shallow bowl)

Heat oil in heavy skillet. Cut eggplant slices into 3/4-inch strips. Dip in
egg; then in bread crumbs. Place eggplant strips into hot fat; turn until
brown on all sides. Using tongs, remove browned eggplant to an oven-safe
plate lined with paper towel to absorb excess oil. Keep warm in a low oven
until all eggplant is cooked.

~~~~~~~~~~~~~~~~~~~~

# SAVORIES

*The French call dessert "bonne bouche" or happy mouth. Perfect!*

## CHOCOLATE FONDUE

*The hot Cointreau can be a villain.*

Melt three large Hershey bars (no nuts) on stove or in microwave. Stir in
1/2 cup Cointreau liqueur. Pour into fondue pot; place over Sterno.

Dipping choices: banana chunks (bite size), pieces of day-old pound cake,
strawberries, apple  wedges, marshmallows.

~~~~~~~~~~~~~~~~~~~~~~

## FRUIT DIP - DELICIOUS SUMMER TREAT

Whip together small container marshmallow fluff with a package of
cream cheese.
Dipping choices: strawberries, large  grapes, chunks of pineapple

~~~~~~~~~~~~~~~~~~~~~

## PEACH BLUEBERRY CRISP

*Kay loves to pick blueberries and peaches. I do the cooking; she
licks the bowl. We make a good team!*

3 cups fresh peaches (peel, pit, slice)   2 tsp. lemon juice
3/4 cup fresh blueberries   4 Tbsp. sugar   3 Tbsp. brandy (optional)
1/2 tsp. cinnamon   1/4 tsp. nutmeg   3/4 cup quick-cook oats
1/4 cup light brown sugar (firmly packed)   3 Tbsp. flour   3 Tbsp. butter

Mix peaches & lemon juice - combine with blueberries, sugar, brandy, spices.
Put this mixture in a 9-in. square pan - set aside. In a bowl combine oats,
brown sugar, flour - cut in butter til well blended. Sprinkle evenly over
peach/blueberry mix. Bake at 350$^0$ for 45 minutes.

~~~~~~~~~~~~~~~~~~~~~

# CHOCOLATE BREAD PUDDING

*An old home recipe from Kay's mother. A delicious variation of the standard.*

1 1/2 cups soft bread crumbs
Blend in: 1 cup milk    1/4 cup sugar + 1 egg (beaten together)
1/8 tsp. salt    1/4 cup cocoa (mix with 3 Tbsp. hot water)    1/2 tsp. vanilla

Place in a baking dish in pan of hot water (1-inch deep). Bake at
350⁰ for 40-45 minutes. Serve hot topped with vanilla ice cream.

~~~~~~~~~~~~~~~~~~~~~~

# GRASSHOPPER PIE

*This is dessert fit for company. The distinct mint flavor is particularly
smooth after a big dinner.*

16 oreo cookies    4 Tbsp. butter, melted    24 large marshmallows
3/4 cup milk    2 oz. crème de menthe    1 cup whipping cream

Make crust by combining crushed oreos & butter. Chill in a 9-in. pie pan.
Make filling by melting marshmallows & milk in a double boiler. Let mix cool
thoroughly - blend in crème de menthe. Fold in whipped cream. Pour into
crust. Garnish with mint leaves & 2 more crushed oreos. Chill 2 hours.

~~~~~~~~~~~~~~~~~~~~~~

# PUMPKIN CHIP COOKIES

*Moist and delicious, these are a unique combination of ingredients. Good
served with coffee ice cream.*

1/3 cup shortening    1 1/3 cups sugar    2 eggs    14 1/2-oz. can pumpkin
1 tsp. vanilla    1 tsp. cinnamon    1 tsp. allspice    12-oz. bag chocolate chips
1/2 cup chopped nuts (optional)    2 1/2 cups Bisquick

Cream shortening & sugar; beat in eggs. When mix is smooth - add pumpkin
& vanilla - stir together. Sift Bisquick & spices together; mix into wet ingredients; add chocolate chips & nuts. Drop by teaspoonful on greased cookie
sheet. Bake at 400⁰ for about 15 minutes.  Makes 5 dozen.

~~~~~~~~~~~~~~~~~~~~~~

# POWER LUNCHES

*Kay and I rise routinely at 5 a.m. and keep a steady pace all day. Breaking
for an hour at noon is a ritual. We often enjoy one of these lunches.*

## EGG SALAD & BOILED HAM POCKETS

Kay makes her egg salad with a little sweet pickle relish, minced onion
(she's an avid mincer!) and mayonnaise. If I make egg salad it has a dash
Gulden's mustard & garlic powder with the mayo.    We like whole wheat
pitas and really pack in the egg salad and layer on two thin slices of
boiled ham. Edible garnish such as bread & butter pickle chips or carrot
sticks always accompany our sandwich.

~~~~~~~~~~~~~~~~~~~~~~~

## APPLES WITH SHARP CHEESE OR PEANUT BUTTER

We each have our own apple and cut it in wedges to the size we prefer.
We enjoy extra sharp cheddar or smoked cheese with this fruit.
Peanut butter spread on apple wedges is also especially delicious when
accompanied by sesame rounds or bread sticks. This is a tremendous
source of energy and just right to get us off
and running for the afternoon's work.

~~~~~~~~~~~~~~~~~~~~~~~

## TOMATO CHEDDAR SOUP & COLE SLAW

Campbell's Cream of Tomato Soup is one of the best comfort foods I know.
We put two tablespoons of grated cheddar cheese in the bottom of a bowl,
then pour in the hot soup. It's just the thing; especially on a cool, rainy day.
Kay makes wonderful cole slaw. You can actually see her juices flowing as she
shreds cabbage, grates carrots, and chops red onion. She mixes the onion with
a little Hidden Ranch Cole Slaw dressing; adds lemon pepper, celery salt,
yogurt and a tablespoon of pineapple juice. She says the order in which the
dressing ingredients are assembled is very important - (I'll never question
anyone who can panel and shiplap walls). I think the secret is the can of
crushed pineapple that she puts in last of all.

~~~~~~~~~~~~~~~~~~~~~~~

# POTLUCK OR CHURCH SUPPER

*During my days at the Fitzwilliam Inn, my husband's advice
was often sought by women faced with preparing quantity meals
for church suppers or fund-raisers.
Once when asked how much turkey was needed to feed 100
people, he replied "10 25-pound turkeys". Then, as an
afterthought added, "or <u>one</u> 250-pounder!"*

## BEEF AND PEA

*This is an ideal casserole to take to a potluck supper. It will serve
eight people and can be easily multiplied if a larger amount is wanted.*

Brown 2 pounds hamburger in a large skillet; drain well.
<u>Add the following:</u>  I can stewed tomatoes    I pkg. onion gravy mix
4 onions, quartered    2/3 cup uncooked rice    2 cups water
I pkg. frozen peas (add when rice done)

Stir together well; simmer til rice is tender. Approximate cooking
time is 20 minutes. When rice is done, add frozen peas; add salt
& pepper to taste. Simmer til peas are soft.

~~~~~~~~~~~~~~~~~~~~~~~~

# CAMPGROUND MEALS

*We prepare a lot of foods at home for our camping trips, then store them in airtight containers for freshness. Food from home that travels along with us adds a special comfort to the trip.*

## KAY'S GRANOLA

*This is a high-energy, lo-cal food supplement that we eat as a snack, put on fruit, cereal or ice cream; and mix into yogurt. Can travel in tightly covered jar or in small, sealed packets.*

1/2 cup honey    1/2 cup safflower oil    7 cups oats    3 cups oat bran

Lightly oil two 15x10 pans. Heat honey & oil in saucepan over med. heat; stir to blend. Mix oats & oat bran in large bowl - drizzle with honey/oil mix. Stir until well-coated. Spread in the two pans. Bake at 250° for 1 hour - stir 3 times during baking time. Cool; refrigerate. Makes 10 cups.

~~~~~~~~~~~~~~~~~~~~~~~~~

## TWO-BEAN & RICE SALAD

3 cups brown rice, unsalted    1 15-oz. can black beans, rinsed & drained
1 15-oz. can pinto beans, rinsed & drained    1 10-oz. pkg. frozen peas, thawed
1 med. red onion, chopped    1/2 cup cilantro, snipped & packed
2/3 cup Lite Caesar salad dressing

Cook rice day ahead; chill overnight. Combine all other ingredients & mix with rice; add salad dressing; stir well. Best if flavors are allowed to blend a few hours before serving.

~~~~~~~~~~~~~~~~~~~~~~~~~

## CAMPER'S EGGS

*This recipe is a great success whether cooking over an open fire, on a fancy grill, or at the RV's gas stove. Handy to know if it's raining and you are not hooked up to electricity.*

<u>Per person:</u>  1 slice bread    1 egg    Butter or oleo

Butter both sides of the bread; cut a round hole in the center about the size of an egg yolk; put bread (and bread hole piece) in frying pan; break egg over the hole. When underside is brown, flip bread to cook egg to desired doneness. (If sunnyside up is desired, flip bread <u>before</u> breaking egg into hole.) Put "hole" on top of egg before serving.

~~~~~~~~~~~~~~~~~~~~~~~~~~

## KIELBASA FRUIT KABOBS

*This is Kay's absolute favorite cookout dish when we're settled in our campsite. It's easier to fix than it looks, so don't pass it up.*

1 pound kielbasa, cut into bite-size slices
1 green pepper, cut in squares
1 can pineapple chunks
1 1/2 tsp. Dijon mustard    3 Tbsp. apricot preserves
Bamboo skewers (soak 30 min. ahead of cooking kabobs)

<u>Glaze:</u> stir together mustard and preserves.

<u>Kabobs:</u> assemble on skewers; alternating kielbasa, peppers and fruit. Brush kabobs with half of the glaze. Grill over medium heat for 5 minutes. Turn kabobs and brush with remaining glaze. Grill 5 more minutes.

~~~~~~~~~~~~~~~~~~~~~~~~~~

# SUNRISE CHAMPAGNE BREAKFAST

*Champagne with Angostura Bitters*
*Scrambled Eggs Parmesan*
*Biscuits*

~~~~~~

*The tradition of having champagne for Sunday breakfast in the summer at the lake dates back to my earliest days at the cabin when the place first became a reality. I felt an urge to celebrate the incredible fact that I had built the cabin from my own resources and owed not a penny on it. Sunday mornings were a time to relax and be good to myself. When Kay became a partner in my life, she immediately embraced the champagne tradition. Serve this meal - outside on a deck where you can salute the sunrise or - in front of a warm fire on chilly mornings. This menu has never deviated from the original.*

## Champagne Cocktail
I use a champagne saucer. I know that flutes contain the bubbles and freshness longer, but there's something more glamorous about the way one holds a saucer as opposed to a flute. Anyway the flutes force my mouth into an uncomfortable shape making it difficult to get a satisfactory mouthful of the bubbly.

3 healthy shakes of Angostura bitters
3 ounces of a good champagne

~~~~~~~~~~~~~~~~~~~~~

## Scrambled Eggs Parmesan (for four people)
Whisk together the following:
   4 eggs   I Tbsp. skim milk per egg   1/4 cup grated Parmesan cheese
      1/2 tsp. garlic powder   Grated fresh black pepper to taste

Scramble in pan sprayed with PAM.

~~~~~~~~~~~~~~~~~~~~~~~~

## Baking Powder Biscuits
I use Bisquick and follow the recipe for rolled biscuits. They're as good as any I've ever tasted. The secret is in the kneading, butting them against one another on the baking pan and allowing them to rise a bit on top of the warm oven before baking.

~~~~~~~~~~~~~~~~~~~

SPECIAL MAIL-IN OFFER

FROM

## KALM PUBLISHING

**...OFFER NOT GOOD IN BOOK STORES...**

ANY EARLIER TITLES
BY AUTHOR
MARY LOU FULLER
**$13.00** (INCLUDING POSTAGE)
(REGULAR PRICE $14.95)

A HORSE IN THE LADIES' ROOM

WHERE LAME DONKEYS LIE

ON THE WINGS OF A UNICORN

| QTY | TITLE | PRICE/BOOK | TOTAL |
|-----|-------|------------|-------|
|     |       |            |       |
|     |       |            |       |
|     |       |            |       |

TOTAL ORDER_____ $............

NAME_____

ADDRESS_____

TELEPHONE_____

E-MAIL_____

**MAIL WITH CHECK TO:**   KALM PUBLISHING

**QUESTIONS?**

KALM Publishing
149 East Side Drive
Concord, NH 03301
uniqueyankee@comcast.net